A
WARM
MOIST
SALTY
GOD

Women Journeying Towards Wisdom

EDWINA GATELEY

———

SOURCE BOOKS
TRABUCO CANYON CALIFORNIA

Library of Congress Cataloging–in–Publication Data
Gateley, Edwina.
A warm, moist, salty God : women journeying towards wisdom /
Edwina Gateley.
      p.   cm.
  Includes bibliographical references.
  ISBN 0-940147-26-2 (pbk.)
  1. Christian women—Religious life. 2. Spirituality.
3. Feminism—Religious aspects—Christianity. 4. Wisdom—
Religious aspects—Christianity. I. Title.
BV4527.G384   1993
248.8'43—dc20   93–11919
                                           CIP

ISBN 0-940147-26-2

Published by:

Source Books
P.O. Box 794
Trabuco Canyon CA 92678

Printed and bound in the USA by KNI Inc.

DEDICATION

For My Son, Niall Kizito.

May he grow in wisdom and grace,

strength and gentleness.

May he care for male and female,

for this earth

and for all living creatures

May he become truly a son of Godde.†

---

† During a recent visit to New Zealand, I stayed with a community of the Sisters of the Mission. Their prayer and hymn book uses the name *Godde*. Having personally struggled with 'God' (as all-male) and 'Goddess' (as all-female) and finding neither word appropriate to my understanding of the Divine, I was delighted to come across a word which embraces both male and female and is rooted in an English far older than our current usage.

MY GRATEFUL THANKS GO TO THE
WHEATON FRANCISCAN SISTERS, ILLINOIS,
AND THE ST. JOSEPH FOUNDATION, KANSAS,
FOR THE FINANCIAL HELP THEY GAVE
WHICH ENABLED ME TO TAKE THE TIME
TO WRITE THIS BOOK.

CONTENTS

O God, accept us
  and do not throw us away.
O God, place us in your navel
  and do not take us out again.
O God, place us in the flame of your womb
  and do not take us out of it.
O God, place us in the folds of your black garment
  and do not take us out of them.
O God, place us in the whiteness of your womb
  and do not take us out again.
O God, place us under your wings
  and do not put us down again.
O God, carry us under your sweet armpits
  and do not put us down again.
O God, carry us on your back
  and do not put us down again.

A MAASAI SONG
TRANSLATED BY JAN VOSHAAR MHM

A POINT OF DEPARTURE

There's a lot going on in our world that is frightening the life and spirit out of many folks. It's hard to find much to rejoice about, although lots of people quietly and desperately try to create private havens of consolation and diversion—going shopping, taking a few drinks, visiting the kids, planning a get-away-from-it-all vacation—all the while guiltily turning off the news and averting their eyes from the newspaper headlines. Truth is, things are in a mess, and they don't seem to be getting any better.

I was appalled to learn that eighty-five per cent of the prison inmates in the United States of America were abused as children, and that we have more people locked up than any other nation in the world. It bothers me that our response to destructive behavior (almost always the result of some kind of childhood abuse) is either the lethal injection or locking people (including children) in cages for many years. More women are raped in America than in any other nation—one in three, to be exact. That's terrifying! Women are constantly looking over their shoulders in fear of being mugged or raped. Ten of us are battered to death each day. No wonder there's a paralytic depression hanging in our polluted air. It's enough to drive one to look for any kind of cover, curl up in the fetal position and hope that there will be a turn for the better.

The turn for the better, however, will only come about when each one of us, hungry for something more, dares to move forward from our despair and paralysis and goes out in search of that better life for ourselves, and ultimately, for our children. Whatever that 'moving out' may look like or feel like for each one as an individual, the journey must be taken. Women today are becoming especially conscious of the call to embark on the journey, and they are becoming more and more aware that it is, indeed, for all of us a matter of life and death.

The Woman in Black

Once upon a time, I spent three months of solitude and prayer in the Sahara Desert in North Africa. For a few weeks of this blessed and silent time, I lived in a tiny shack-cave built into the mountainside of part of the Sahara that resembled what I had seen of the moon's surface on television. A few days before the end of the retreat, I checked the tin well that was sunk into the earth, and realized that the water had just about run dry. It appeared that I had no option but to sit around and hope that I wouldn't die of thirst. I could eke out the little that I had and wait...

But another possibility suddenly, and rather disturbingly presented itself. I could look for water! On reflection, the idea really was quite absurd. After all, I was in the vast desert with no life in sight for dozens of miles, apart from beetles, snakes and the odd tarantula. It was ridiculous. But... it *would* be nice to have water. It would be good to know that I could relax and not worry because I was safe and provided for.

I reflected on the two possibilities before me, and I realized with a terrible sense of responsibility that the decision to look for water could only be made by me, *had* to be made by me. It felt like—it *was*— an undeniably irrational and futile thought, to make a journey that, in the circumstances, surely was doomed to failure. I was surrounded by hundreds of miles of sand and barren volcanic rock. How could I imagine finding water in such a place! Nevertheless, I took out my tin can, noted the position of the sun, and began to walk into the wilderness.

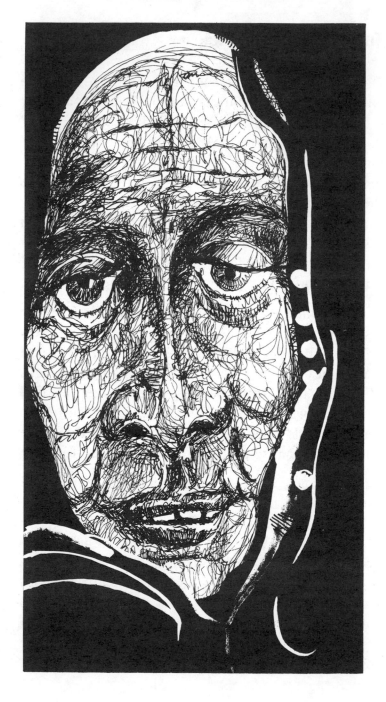

As I trudged along, my rational brain was insistently reminding me, "How silly you are, this is so stupid..." But something else in me was smiling and feeling free and strong. I thought about God and all the times I had been exhorted to trust and to believe in miracles. I thought about how rarely we are actually involved in miracles, and I wondered if a lack of faith and trust was indeed the reason why the world and our lives seemed to be lacking in miracles—in Good News, in awareness of God-with-Us. And then I said to myself, "So why not? Why on this wild journey of hope should there not be a miracle?"

I nearly gave up as the sun rose higher. And I nearly turned back as my rational brain continued to plague me with scornful thoughts of how silly and irresponsible this journey was. I kept going. Over three miles I walked until suddenly, there in the distance, shimmering through veils of heat, I saw a tiny shack made of stones and covered in goat-skin. A mirage? From within the shack emerged a figure, tall, wild, dressed in a long black gown with a black veil around her head. A woman in the desert!

Excited, I ran towards her, and she to me. Then, with only a few hundred feet between us, we both stopped. Like animals stalking prey, we cautiously, slowly continued to move towards each other. She was an Arab of the Tuareg tribe, desert wanderers, and apparently lived alone in her squat shelter, far from other habitation. She was burnt brown with the sun, her dark eyes were deep and wise and her face criss-crossed with a thousand crevices. I was amazed to come across another human being in these desolate sands. For what seemed a long time we stared in utter astonishment into each other's eyes.

Then, wordless, but smiling all over her brown, cracked face, the woman took my hand and led me to her shelter. There she placed a hand-woven rug on the sand and motioned me to sit. She disappeared into a cluster of nearby rocks. So I sat alone, still dumbfounded at encountering another woman in this barren place.

Eventually she returned, carrying a pot of hot liquid and two earthenware mugs. She had brewed sweet Arabian tea! Together we sat, two women brought together from two worlds apart, sipping tea and relishing the wonder of the other's presence. Our languages differed, our worlds, our lives were different, but I knew, and I felt she did too, that our Gods were one and the same. As we shared the warm, refreshing tea, we also shared the God who sat with us in that wild, miraculous place. It was the same God who brought me into the wilderness, there to speak to my soul.

The woman stood and took me again by the hand. She led me through the rocks to where a deep pool of water lay, cradled between huge boulders. I filled my tin can and then embraced the black-clad woman with the deep, wise eyes, who had given me tea and water. On parting, we waved. We would never meet again. I was deeply moved. Stirred into awe by a miracle.

I had taken the journey against all rationale and common-sense. I had gone into the desert with a little bit of faith and a little bit of hope, looking for water. We shall never know the miracles that God has waiting for us until we take the journey that leads into the wilderness.

TEA IN THE DESERT

Wandering, alone, through the desert.
Sun shrieking heat,
Sweat pouring and dripping,
Rocks, barren and hostile
Sheltering
The brave desert flower.
And I—solitary beating heart
In a vast and empty land
Wandering, wandering, seeking
A lost and lonely God.

Beyond the rocks
A smell of goats
Hanging thick and sweet
In the still air.
And there, standing defiant against
A thousand miles of sand,
A woman
Burnt brown, clad
In sweeping black and
Colored beads.

We walk to meet,
To cross
The centuries and the nations.
Eyes, black, shining a lost
And ancient wisdom
Speaking the naked horrors
And splendor of
Uncompromising solitude.

Smile. No words.
Shattering the barriers of language.
Hands touch,
Brown and cracked,
White and smooth,
Clasping and joining
A thousand cultures.

Walk together to her home
A rough and sturdy shelter
Of rocks and goatskins.
Squat on Tuareg rug laid out
Proudly on the sand.
Smile. No words.
Eyes, searching, speaking
A million unknown words.
Tea. Thick, hot, sweet
Prepared with love and care
In an old tin kettle
On an open fire.
Sip. Smile gratitude.
Smile. No words.
Woman of the desert.
Woman of the West.
The world brought together.
Peace and harmony established.
Rivalry and hate abolished.
Black and white.
The lion and the lamb.
Smile. No words.
Tuareg woman.
English woman.
Sharing the Kingdom
Sipping tea
In the vast and lonely desert
With a found and
Living God.

PSALMS OF A LAYWOMAN

THE WOMAN WHO TOUCHED DEEPLY

Many years ago, there was a woman who cried almost all the time. According to Christian scriptures, this poor woman had a hemorrhage. The scripture writers were really a bit hung-up about women's bodies and natural functions, so, instead of saying what the real problem was, they said she had a hemorrhage. What was really happening was that the woman had a gynecological problem which resulted in ongoing menstruation. For twelve years she had been menstruating.

Now, just imagine! Four or five days a month is bad enough, but *twelve years!* In the culture and custom of that time, a woman who was menstruating was considered unclean. She was treated like some people treat AIDS sufferers today: alienated from society, the community. If a menstruating woman touched another person, it was believed she could communicate uncleanness to the other. So the woman had to withdraw, as is still the custom in some tribal societies. She had to retreat from the community until her period was over.

The woman spent a fortune on gynecologists, medical insurance and doctor's visits. She cashed all her savings and bonds to try to solve her problem. But nothing worked. Nothing worked! And so, for twelve years she stayed in her corner. She had her own cup, her own saucer, her own plate, (lest she contaminate others). And there she was. Ostracized.

One day, she heard on the grapevine that there
was a man going around. JESUS was his name. He
was saying to the blind, "You can see." He was
saying to the lame, "You can walk." And he was
even raising the dead! The woman heard these rumors
and her heart began to beat faster. She was excited
because, all of a sudden, she glimpsed the possibility
of healing and wholeness. "Maybe even for me..."
she mumbled to herself. And her dulled eyes began
to shine.

Then she remembered the reality. "Oh no, how
could I, how dare I imagine that me, little nobody,
could go out there and reach for dignity, for fullness
and for wholeness?" And she accepted the way it
was, she accepted the status quo, she accepted what
they told her. And she stayed in her corner.

But guess what? It wouldn't go away. It was
something in her belly-button, a deep gut instinct
behind her belly-button. Something deep inside her
kept stirring and nudging her until one day, she took
her hat, put it on and said "I'm off!" She opened the
door and out she came from her corner.

And there, outside, were all the crowds of people
gathered around Jesus of Nazareth, saying "Oh, the
Great One, the Guru, the Prophet, the Leader!" The
woman knew she was taking her life in her hands, because
if they discovered her, if they recognized who this was,
wandering around in public, they could punish her, even
kill her for breaking the law, for coming out of her
place, for daring to move forward, reaching out for
something more than what she had and was.

She went right on through the crowd, in and out, weaving like a woman who knows how to weave. She went through the hostile crowd, kept on going, until suddenly she found herself right up near the front. Imagine the cheeky, pushy woman! How dare she! But, she *did*. She got right up to the front and bumped into the disciples of Jesus. They were standing in front of The Master, surrounding him to protect and guard him, keeping the crowds away from the sacred place, the sacred person. "Stand back!" They shouted. But this determined lady ignored their barking order. Her dream was now too important, too driving to abandon. She slipped right between the legs of the disciples until she was face to face with Jesus.

She had done it! She had taken the journey and she knew she didn't have to give a homily or a speech, or anything fancy. As a woman she knew the power of touch. She leaned forward and reached out to touch the hem of the garment woven by his mother. And as she did so, suddenly the power came from Jesus into the woman. ZIP! Startled, he turned and said, "Who was that who touched me?" And the disciples (who never knew what was going on at the best of times and were always the last to understand) missed it.

Jesus said, "Somebody touched me." The disciples were amused by his apparent naivete, and said,
"Well, everybody's here, everybody's touching you."
"No, no. You don't understand," replied Jesus,

"Someone here knows what's going on at a deeper level." Knowing it was her, the woman came forward and said,

"It's me."

Jesus looked at her, amazed at the risky journey he knew she had taken. He stared at her and smiled. "Woman," he said " Stand up!" And the woman who, for twelve years had been bent double, bowed down by her so-called disease, by her inadequacy, by her diminishment, for the first time in twelve years, at the command of Jesus of Nazareth, stood up straight. And Jesus declared, "Woman, your faith has made you whole!"

Ah! What it must have been like for the woman, after all the time she had spent in the corner thinking she was nothing, nobody—to then hear the words of Jesus: "Stand up!"

Why, she was a new woman! All because she heard the word and took a risk for wholeness. It was the journey that healed her, that called her to a whole new way of being. So, what did she do then? She didn't creep back to where she had come from and say to herself, "Oh, what a nice experience." No, something magical had happened in her belly. She could never be the same. From then on she walked around saying, "Look what happened to me! I can stand up straight. I have seen the dream and the vision. Nobody will bow me down again!"

And there was a light in her eye. This light was seen by others who were bowed down, as she once had been. The little lady, now undaunted, began to say to others:

"Stand up! It's okay. I know about the journey, you see. Stand up!"

Yes. That is what women today must do. They must come out of their corners, their darknesses and their fears. They must take the life-risking journey, however hostile the crowds. The women who make that journey, impelled by the gut-instinct for wholeness within, know with a painful awareness that no-one should be bowed down, no-one should be hungry, homeless or cold. We know these things in our bellies. But each must make her own journey before she can walk with others. Then we can go and tell the Good News to our brothers and sisters, that God is with us, that all of us must ultimately stand up if we are to birth God's Kingdom on Earth.

There, where the forest fell

dark and deep

there was no path.

So I trod one.

Midwives

Something happens when women begin to stand up and reach out for wholeness, justice and dignity. The boat begins to rock. The system begins to shift and to change when women, the powerful force of the feminine, stand up and commit themselves to new ways of being. Slowly the world begins to change as women refuse to stay in the kitchens, on the back rows and in the bedrooms, while our children are raped, our sisters jailed and our daughters pimped.

For centuries, women, in one way or another, have been standing up against the system and refusing to obey unjust laws. Take the *Book of Exodus*, for example. Everybody has heard of Moses. They tell his story: he is the great prophet, the great leader of the people of Israel. But few people have heard of Shipra and Puah. Shipra and Puah, who are they? What is *their* story? And what does it say to women today?

In the time when the people of Israel were imprisoned and enslaved in Egypt, Pharaoh looked at the Hebrew people and saw their numbers multiplying. And he said, "We can't have this. If there's any more of them, they might rebel. We have to control the crowds, we have to keep their numbers down."

So Pharaoh called Shipra and Puah, the midwives of the people of Israel. The King of Egypt said to them, "Every time a Hebrew woman gives birth to a baby, I want you, if it is a boy, to strangle it."

"Yes sir," said the Hebrew midwives, Shipra and Puah, and went about their midwiving business. Time passed and the King of the Egyptians watched and observed. The people continued to increase in number. The King began to think, "What happened to Shipra and Puah and my orders?" So he called them.

"I ordered you to destroy the male babies of the Hebrews!" And Shipra and Puah said,

"Oh, do you know, sir, lord, king, it's very, very difficult because every time we get a call from a woman in labor, we *rush* there. But these Hebrew women are *so* strong and tough, by the time we get there, the babies have been already delivered, and we are too late to intercept the birth!"

Ah, women can find a way to get around unjust laws! Dodging, weaving, if necessary finding a way that may not involve direct confrontation. Shipra and Puah did not obey oppressive laws. They outsmarted the King and his law. So Moses was born. His mother, seeing that he was a boy, took him and said, "I must hide him."

She made a basket for him, and put him in the river. Then she called her daughter, Miriam. And Miriam watched the child in the waters of the Nile. The daughter of Pharaoh came by the river and saw the baby in the basket, and said, "I will take care of him secretly."

And so Moses, the great liberator, the great leader of the people, was born and was nurtured because five women conspired quietly in the background to save him: Shipra, Puah, the mother of Moses, Miriam his sister and the daughter of the Pharaoh.

They say that behind every great man there is a great woman. If those women had not quietly but courageously worked together, we never would have heard of Moses. Yet we have been told only *his* story, not the stories of the women. We need to know the significant roles played by the women who have gone before us –those powerful ladies in our history and in scriptures. They have made a difference. We must not be allowed to forget it.

MARY THE POLITICALLY INCORRECT

The first great miracle worked by Jesus was at the wedding feast at Cana. There was a party, a wedding party, and everybody was there. There was Jesus, having a few drinks with his friends at the bar. His mother was there too, with all the other women, having a good time. Mary, being a woman, also kept her eye on the coffee table and on the bar counter, because women think about practicalities like that. Women instinctively are concerned about hospitality and making sure there is enough food and drink for everyone.

Mary saw that the wine was going down. Nobody else noticed it. The guys were drinking and cracking jokes, sharing their war stories or whatever. But Mary noticed it. She went up to her boy, Jesus, tapped him on the shoulder and said, "Son, they're running out of wine."

What the woman did was politically incorrect according to the custom and culture of that community. An adult female was not permitted to address an adult male in public. It was simply unacceptable! Women were to remain silent and keep to themselves. Here was this woman who dared to go right up to her son in front of all his friends and say, "Hey, they've not got enough wine."

And Jesus was mortally embarrassed and offended. He knew his mother was out of line. Humiliated, he turned to her, "Woman, what is that to thee or me? My time has not yet come." He was thinking, "How dare you. How dare you talk to me in public, embarrassing me in front of my friends!" And the rest of the guys were all trying to look as if they didn't know what was going on, probably feeling glad that she wasn't *their* mother! Mary, knew the power of motherhood, and that the important thing was not the regulations, nor what was acceptable or unacceptable, but whether people were celebrating and having a good time. She turned from Jesus and called the waiter. "Waiter, come here. Do what he says."

Jesus was mortified by his mother's obstinacy. Because of her, he had to make a choice. He could have zapped his mother right then and there, and from the point of view of etiquette and custom, he would have been within his rights. He could have put her in her place and he would have been respected for taking a stand against the woman's impudence. His culture would have him say, "Mother, get lost." But Jesus did not.

The beauty of Jesus of Nazareth was his openness to 'the other.' He would try to understand the other side. Listening to his mother, he could see that she had a point. So, he said to the waiter, "Bring me water." At the call of his mother, who recognized the precedence of hospitality over rules, he changed the water into wine and gave the people what they wanted so they could celebrate.

Too often we are caught up and paralyzed by some bureaucratic system that does not allow for flexibility or creativity. We are squeezed and squashed into ways of doing and being that are unhealthy and unwholesome. Women today must begin to look for creative alternatives which free the human spirit from those oppressive customs and systems that now must be questioned. It will require a great deal of lateral thinking! Women and children have a different perspective on things and can give us another side of a situation. We must be open to that flexibility.

Once there was a religious education teacher, who would read the children stories from the scriptures, and then she would say, "Okay kids, off you go home." The next day, when they returned she would ask the children to tell in their own words the story she had read. There was a little fellow named Billy. The teacher had read the story of the wedding feast at Cana. She said to Billy, "Okay Billy, can you tell me the story of that wedding?" And little Billy said,

"Well, there was this here party and there was Jesus and there was his mom having a ball. Then there was no wine left, so Mary went to Jesus an sez to him, 'Hey son, they ain't got no wine.' And Jesus sez to his mom, 'Well hell, it ain't my party!'"

Sometimes, perhaps, we need to loosen up and allow ourselves to see our stories from a different and more imaginative perspective.

THE JOHN

The fact that women were excluded from scriptures does not mean that they were not there. On the contrary, they were very much there. Looking at the story of the Feeding of the Five Thousand (Matthew 14) we read:

> Those who ate numbered about five thousand men, to say nothing of women and children.

My question is: how many would have been fed if they *had* counted women and children? —Six thousand? Ten thousand? Fifteen? At that time and in that culture, there was no counting the females. Only men were counted and later recorded.

We have inherited an entire documentation of history and scripture which rarely includes the feminine. Women's stories have been largely omitted, limited or lost in the Christian tradition and history which has been passed down to us. We have to begin to retrieve our stories, and to re-read scriptures from the perspective of what it might really have been like if women had been included.

Women have to speak aloud. We must no longer allow our voices to be muted. We have to question and confront. Yet women don't need to be destructive in order to be whole. We *do* have to challenge where there is distortion, or where there are lies, or where there is deceit and oppression.

I work with women in prostitution, and am familiar with a few of the brothels in Chicago. The men come into the brothels and they choose the

24

women they want to have sex with. One day, I was involved in a meeting at a big hospital in Chicago. The purpose of the meeting was to try to get more medical funds for the very poor. It was attended by rather important and significant people, and one of these people was the vice-president of the hospital, pin-stripe suit, very much a respected man in the community. He came and sat down opposite me. I looked at him, then looked at him again and said to him,

"Don't I know you? Haven't I seen you somewhere before?"

"No, I don't know you."

"Oh," I said, "I'm sure I recognize you. I have seen you before."

"Oh no, no," said he as he backed away.

You know how it is when you've got something on the tip of your tongue and you just can't remember it? I went home wondering... I was sure I had seen that face somewhere... I remembered it that night as I was going to sleep. This man goes to the brothel every Thursday afternoon.

Ah, women must say —*What* are you doing there? Why are you abusing our sisters? And why is it kept so quiet? Women have to give voice to that which is hidden, to that which is being denied and covered up. If society insists on criminalizing and jailing our sisters in prostitution, it must criminalize and jail our brothers too.

In the book *I Hear A Seed Growing*, I wrote a poem about this.

THE PEROXIDE HOOKER

Down the alley
The peroxide hooker
Dove furtively in search of a quick job
For five bucks.
(Used to be ten but times are hard
And we can't be choosey.)
The decoy cop cruised up
And beckoned to
The peroxide hooker,
To hassle for the price
And the service to be given...
She shot for ten and then,
In desperation... five.
The badge was flashed
And spitting and snarling,
To bite back tears,
The peroxide hooker was
Bundled in the back seat
And sped triumphantly
To the big red jail we built for her.
We put prison bars around her,
And high tiled walls
So we would not see
The peroxide hooker cry and spit on us
In grief turned to fury
And pain turned to hate.
We nailed her to our public cross
And, shaking our heads, tutting her sin,
We left the hooker to die alone
In the shame she was born in.
We turned away
From the peroxide hooker
And fled to the dark safety
Of the sacred church walls
To pray for God's mercy
For the woman on the cross.

LICE

I once worked in a downtown overnight shelter. It was a big basement shelter, and every night when the homeless came in, I would stand at the door handing out old blankets. Once, this guy came up to me, "Edwina, could I have one without lice?"

"What?" I said.

"Could I have one that doesn't have any lice in it? And one that's got no urine on it?" And I said,

"Oh, er... okay." And started holding up the blankets to see if I could get one without lice. "Here, I've got one here. This one's got no lice. There's nothing moving on this one."

And suddenly I thought to myself, "What am I doing? Here am I picking out blankets without lice and urine for certain folks. This is all wrong." So, I went to the supervisor and I said to him, "This is not right, we should launder these blankets every day instead of every week. We can't do this to these folks. They deserve better than this." The supervisor looked at me and smiled, he shook his head and said,

"Edwina, let me tell you something. When you have been here as long as I have, you get used to it."

UUUH... something in me screamed. We must *never* get used to it! We must never accept the way things are because we are told 'Well, it's always been like this.' This world was not meant to be like this! We were not meant to live in poverty. We were not meant to be hungry. We were not meant to be homeless. We were not meant to sleep in lice-infested blankets. When we accept the system with our 'this is the way it is,' we become part of it. We are part of the oppression, the injustice, the diminishment.

Blessed are they who never get used to it!

Women must refuse to get used to poverty and homelessness and oppression and war. We must give birth to something better for our children, and we must begin by challenging those in power and authority. We must not be afraid to demand and claim a better way, a better life. We must speak as the Syrophonecian woman did in the gospel...

Jesus had been preaching all week. He'd been giving retreats and he was really tired because he couldn't get through to the people. Jesus always had a hard time getting through to his own family and community. His own people. In contemporary terms you might say that the 'good folk' were the problem, because they did not really understand or accept the Good News. They didn't put the message into practice. Many turned away. And even the disciples said, "We don't understand. Could you explain it in private, please?" They really were a hopeless lot.

Jesus was frustrated. He had reached the point where he needed a break. He needed to get away to sort it all out. So, he withdrew, into the territory of Tyre and Sidon, an area which was alien to Jesus, – the local ghetto, for someone who comes from the suburbs. It was a dive, a foreign place. He found a rundown motel and, according to scripture:

He did not want anyone to know he was there.

Can't blame him really. Naturally enough, Jesus needed some space, just needed to get away from it all, and try to make some sense out of his life and calling.

But, here comes the woman, a Syrophonecian, a foreigner. In contemporary equivalence we might say she was a black prostitute, an unmarried mother, pregnant, on welfare and didn't speak English, –perhaps an illegal immigrant. She was all those things we hesitate to approve, living in a part of town we wouldn't care to wander into. She was unacceptable to Jesus' people too. Seeing him from a distance, she recognized him. She had seen his picture in the paper, on television. "I know who you are! Hey, Jesus!" She cried aloud. "Jesus, Yoo-ooh!"

A very disgruntled Jesus didn't want to see anyone at all that day. The woman yelled, "Ooee, hey I've got a problem. I'm in trouble." And Jesus said,

"No. No, leave me alone." After all, she wasn't from his part of town or even his church.

"But I have this little girl, eleven years old. She's very ill and she's going to die. I know, I know you can do something. Please do something!"

"No! I'm on retreat and I'm praying." He knew she didn't fit into his category. She didn't fit his group. She didn't belong in his BOX. "Leave me alone!"

But the woman pestered and nagged and would not leave, would not go home. Because, you see, she wanted her daughter to live. So even though she did not fit into the appropriate category for Jesus' attention, even though she was nobody, she badgered him. She dared to say to this important, famous person: "Listen to *me!*" And she a nobody. She would not shut up. And Jesus was getting angrier and angrier, because after all, he *was* on retreat. At last, in his anger, he turned to the woman and shouted,

"Woman, is it right to give the bread that is on the table for the children to the dogs? Will you GET LOST!" –Not nice of Jesus of Nazareth to call anyone a dog. The woman turned to him.

"Excuse me, excuse me SIR! But, even the little ones underneath get the crumbs from the table. Don't be forgetting the little ones underneath." And Jesus of Nazareth, who had been caught up in his special agenda, in his retreat, who had focused on his own people, his own community –the people of Israel, was suddenly stretched by the words of the woman:

"What did you say?" He asked.

"Don't forget the little ones," she said again. And Jesus began to see more clearly what was happening to him:

"I'm sorry. I am tired. I got so caught up in my own thing, I lost track of what I am really here to do." He did a turn-about! Just as at the wedding feast at Cana, a woman prodded him into an expanded awareness. It was she, the foreigner, the little one, the nobody who brought Jesus back on track, put him in mind of his mission, his responsibility. And Jesus turned around and said, "Woman, your child is healed."

Jesus had no problem changing his mind when he knew it was the right thing to do. Even Jesus could be stretched beyond his limited vision, by this woman, by the little one. That's the way God operates. God is anxious to empower the voiceless, is longing to raise up those who are bent over. And when those who are bowed down stand up, all sorts of things can happen. If only we dare to move forward. If only we allow ourselves to be transformed by the 'other'—the different—that which we may find hard to understand. The women, the 'little ones,' the ones on the edges, must dare to remind our leaders, our government officials and our bishops, what they need to be about.

Once, when I was sitting in Genesis House, our house of hospitality for women involved in prostitution, there was a knock on the door. I opened it and there was a beautiful blond-haired woman standing on the doorstep. She was tall, shapely, a high-class call-girl and a prostitute. She was crying. "Help me! I want to get off the streets!" Well, of course I opened the door wide and she came in and sat down. I listened to her story of abuse on the streets: incest, violence, rape: all those things that drive so many women to destruction. Her name was Anna. I said,

"Anna, stay with us and you can start a new life!"

"Oh," says Anna, "Start a new life…"

"Yes, you can begin again."

Anna was ecstatic. She came to live with us in our home at Genesis House. But after a few days, I heard the other women whispering, "We don't like her. She doesn't fit in with us. We don't want her living here with us." I was saddened by their lack of acceptance of Anna. But I observed Anna, and called her one day to sit down for a chat.

"Anna, you've not been honest with me, have you?" She shook her head and tears began to fall and she sobbed,

"No."

"Anna, you're a man, aren't you?" Anna nodded and looked at me with tears falling down her face. "Why didn't you tell me who you are?" I demanded.

"If I had told you who I am –a faggot, a queen, a queer, you would *never* have taken me into your house, would you?" I was stunned at the question, stunned at the challenge. I began to reason, to defend.

"Well, you see, Anna, we only work with women –I mean we work with females... I mean..." And my words were saying –you do not belong, you do not fit into our boxes, our categories... "No! I would not have taken you into this house if I had known who you were!"

Ah! The Great Compassionate God says, "My Kingdom is for all! All of them. Gather them up! – Jews and Palestinians. Gays and straights. Black and white. Male and female. Alien and citizen... Love them ALL. I dare you." Our challenging God, our huge, huge God is too big for us! "I dare you to love them all."

"Yes, I know, God," I protest. "But, you see, we have a Holy Catholic Church, a Holy Roman Catholic Church, and we have boxes, and there are certain people, well, I mean you wouldn't really want to have *them* in your Kingdom."

"YES," says this God. "Look what I have birthed. Love all that I have created. They are mine."

Ah! I thought that I was so free. I thought I was a liberated woman. We have far to travel on our journey to God who knows no boundaries, no restrictions, no boxes. The God we end up with will not be the God we started out with.

"Anna, stay with us. We need you." We need you for our own conversion. We need you for our own evangelization. Yes... we must gather them all up. Like a mother who gathers her children.

I had nearly bought into the system. I had been nearly sucked into the way of being that says we have to live with filth and lice, that says 'these people are okay, and these people are not. The acceptable and the unacceptable. We must tell our brothers to set the prisoners free. To receive the transsexuals. To gather up the gay community. To gather up the blacks. To gather up the poor. Raise up the rape victims. Embrace and heal the incest victims. We must tell our brothers that all of them are called to dignity, fullness and wholeness.

We must give birth.

JESUS, SON OF GOD

Jesus, Son of the Living God,
all burnt out and weary
fled to a quiet unknown place
to rave and weep alone,
grieving for a mission tattered
that made folks laugh or gasp
in righteous disapproval.

But the woman saw him slip
like a fugitive into the shadows
and yelled aloud
in delighted recognition
Jesus, Son of God! She cried,
Heal my daughter
sick from birth
and young and black and poor.

The minister turned
stung at the rude intrusion
by foreign female stranger.
Away from me! He cried aloud,
Don't trespass on our private land
this sacred space is ours alone
it's not for you, not for you!
Yelled Jesus, Son of God.

The woman froze in anger
eyes shining with her truth
Your private land and sacred space
is also mine, she said.
The healing is for all of us—
black, rich and poor and white,
remember that! She said to him,
Jesus, Son of God.

The man turned and looked upon her
as understanding seeped his soul.
Oh, woman, I came for you, he said
Not sacred space nor private land.
For black and rich and poor and white
and all humanity.
Your child is healed and whole again
Said Jesus, Son of God.

WHERE ARE MARTHA'S KEYS?

One way or another we have to give birth to the new and bring life where there is death. In the Gospel of John there is the story of Martha. Martha was a homemaker. She was a great cook, terrific in the kitchen. She loved shopping and entertaining, so she was always trying out new recipes for Jesus and his friends. Martha had a sister called Mary. Mary was quiet and introverted, and spent most of her time in the library. She kept a journal and was always going on inner-journey retreats. A quiet little thing. Anyway, Martha and Mary got on well together, and they had a brother who was called Lazarus. They were all great friends of Jesus. So when Jesus was passing through town, he would stop in for one of Martha's special dinners, or for a couple of drinks, or whatever. They had a wonderful relationship.

This is what happened. Lazarus got a bug, a virus and was very sick. Well, Martha who was well organized and liked to get everything under control, sent letters out to friends and family and called up relatives telling them that Lazarus was sick and could they come over and bring some medicine and flowers and stuff.

This was the time when Jesus was running about the country, giving preached retreats and such. So Martha wrote to him, 'Get yourself over here. Lazarus is sick, come over and visit and say a few words to him.' And Jesus, who was off doing this religious thing with his disciples, gets a letter from

Martha, saying, 'Come home. Lazarus is sick.' But Jesus was caught up, you see. Busy. Tied up with clients and talks and schedules. And so he left the letter on his desk. Towards the end of the retreat he remembered it. "I have this feeling we need to get back. We need to go and see how Lazarus is doing," he said to his retreat team. Suddenly he was afraid that Lazarus may not have made it. And he said to his disciples, "Let's move it guys!"

They rushed back, and guess who is waiting for them? –Martha, full of repressed anger and grief, standing there in the cemetery. She saw Jesus coming. She must have looked at her watch and said something like, "Where the hell have you been? I wrote to you two weeks ago. Is our mailing system screwed up or what? Why didn't you come?" According to the gospel of John she continued, "If you had been here Lazarus would not have died!" ('Ah,' says the woman, 'There would not have been a death.') "But even now I know that anything you ask in the name of God will be given to you. For you are the Christ, the Son of God."

And she ran off to fetch her sister Mary from the library. They all gathered with Jesus, standing by the tomb of Lazarus. The message is clear: 'You are the Christ –you can do it. God will give you anything, so DO IT!'

Jesus, looking around at his disciples and seeing the woman standing there in faith and determination, moved forward at Martha's words and cried aloud, "Lazarus, come forth!" And the dead man rose.

Ah, the greatest miracle in the New Testament, the resurrection of the dead. And there was the woman, the homemaker, right in the middle of it. It was the woman who said, "You are the Christ, the Son of the Living God." When Peter, the leading disciple, said the same words Jesus responded, "For this I will give you the keys of the Kingdom of Heaven."

My question is –Where are Martha's keys?

Women need to question why it is that Peter ended up with the keys and the big statue in Rome when Martha said exactly the same thing and wasn't even noticed! What about Martha? Where's her statue? Does she not also have a claim on the keys of the Kingdom? And *Peter,* after proclaiming his faith in Jesus, denied that he knew Jesus at all! Three times, no less. Still, he got the keys and Martha didn't. Some basic unfairness is going on here. The woman stayed faithful to Jesus. I'm not saying discount the man. But let's be fair. There's a similar imbalance in the treatment of the two people caught in prostitution. They arrest the woman but the man goes home to his kids and dinner.

Throughout our history we adopt and maintain double standards. God will have none of it. And that is why God is concerned about raising up the little ones, the children and the child-like who in their powerlessness have a built-in and precise sense of what is just. Through them, God challenges us saying, "Don't let the powerful hold onto their double standards. I will be with you until the very end. You must come forward, come out of your corner and speak for what is right. You must be faithful people."

A New Window

We read in I Corinthians 14:34, that women should not be allowed to speak in church. That such a directive was made at all, indicates that at one time women were *not* silent in church. They were being a nuisance! They were preaching and teaching, speaking in tongues and interpreting. They were being very active in God's church.

They had gathered around Jesus. And we know what women are like. They get into things. They talk and chat and get excited and make a racket. They gather. That is why attendance at almost all our church services and ceremonies is predominantly female. It is the women who do the gathering. It is the women who search for the sacred and the spiritual. The men organize it, and take charge of it, but it is the women who are the seekers.

As they had gathered around Jesus of Nazareth, so the women gathered in small communities, and they were often the community leaders of the young church. It got to the point where the men were beginning to say, "You know, it's getting a bit too much, this. These women are out of control. They are talking too much. Taking over. They are *preaching*, for goodness' sake. These women are becoming a nuisance. We'd better fix it. Let's have a new law. From now on, we have made a new rule: women are going to be quiet in church."

And so we all shut up. –Except the men. Sad really.

41

In Romans 16, Paul writes a letter to one of the churches, introducing Phoebe, a leading figure of the early Christian community.

I commend to you our sister, Phoebe, a Deaconess. Give her a welcome worthy of saints.

Twenty-five years ago, I went to see my local bishop. I said to the bishop, "I would like to be a deaconess." Says the bishop to me:

"But, my dear, we don't have deaconesses."

"Why?"

"Well, my dear, we have never had deaconesses in the Catholic tradition."

"Bishop! You're wrong! Have you not read Romans 16 where Paul introduces Phoebe, a deaconess who is worthy of the welcome of the saints?"

"Well...um...We haven't had deaconesses in a long time..."

Something is missing. What happened to the women? Why were the women repressed? Is it that we spoke too much? Is it that we believed so intensely? Is it that we cared for the children and the little ones? Is it that the men felt threatened by capable women? Really —both men and women have lost out.

In Luke 15, we read the Parable of the Good Shepherd. There was a shepherd and he had a flock of little white lambs, and one little black one. The black one got away. (I always thought the one who got away was the smartest!) The shepherd went after the little black lamb, and gathered it up in his arms. In the scriptures, who is the shepherd? The shepherd is Jesus, the Redeemer, the Lord, the One Who Saves. The shepherd saved the little one. God saves the little ones. We see plenty of representations of the Good Shepherd in books and church windows.

In the same chapter, Luke 15, immediately following this parable, there is another one. It is about a woman in a lounge, and she drops her purse. The purse rolls away and a dime falls out. She looks everywhere for her dime, and eventually she finds it. "Look, look I have found the dime! Celebrate with me!"

Who is the woman in the lounge? –The woman is *God*. But why haven't we seen in the churches, in the stained-glass windows behind the altar, the woman standing there with her purse and her dime? Why haven't we seen her in our religious books and our bibles, sitting on the couch saying, "I've found it!" No. She's not there. But we have seen the shepherd in the stained-glass windows. How is it that we choose the one to the neglect of the other? How many of our children know that the woman standing there with her purse is God the Redeemer? No, we have chosen to have only the male model of the Holy One. No wonder we're unbalanced. No wonder we're bent down.

In Matthew 13, there is a farmer and he is going out to sow. And he sows the seed right and left. Some of the seed falls on rocky ground, some falls on fertile ground. The Sower is God, Redeemer, the One who Sows and Gathers. Haven't we seen in our

BEHOLD ✦ I ✦ HAVE ✦ FOUND ✦ IT ✦ ! ✦

churches, the picture of the Sower in stained-glass? And haven't we seen this parable represented in the Bible and in our religious books?

Following this parable, Jesus told a second. There is a woman in the kitchen wearing her apron and kneading dough. And she kneads, and she kneads, she mixes in the yeast and she puts it in the oven and bakes the bread. And it rises... and it rises.

Who is she? *God*. But why haven't we seen in our holy places and holy books, the pictures of the Woman standing in the kitchen with the loaf of bread? Why not? Who did the selecting? We know who did the selecting, and we know the importance of symbols, illustrations and images. For many centuries, choices have been made that have produced an all-male, white God. And it's nothing to do with the homemaker. It's nothing to do with the baker. It's nothing to do with women.

We wonder why people are sick, we wonder why people are so hungry. And we say to ourselves, "What is missing? Do I need another car? Some more security? –How about those Municipal Bonds?"

There is a deep spiritual hunger in people. Something is missing, and I believe it is the feminine dimension, the wholeness that comes from a God in our bellies who is *everything*—male and female, black and white, dark and light, earth and sky. It is a wholeness that women must encompass, calling it forth in an unbalanced and unjust world. Women must rediscover the feminine side of God if we are to bring some balance back into our churches and into

our lives, and our society. We must refuse to
acknowledge a god whom our brothers have shaped
in their own image and likeness, a god and a
spirituality which condones and endorses all manner
of violence and oppression in the name of order and
power. A god whom our children are not interested
in getting to know.

Do you remember learning about God in school?
The Catechism began like this:
> Who is God?

The answer we all had to learn by heart was:
> God is the Supreme Spirit who alone exists of
> himself and is infinite in all perfections.
> Question: Why did God make you?
> Answer: God made me to know him, love him and
> serve him in this world and to be happy with him
> forever in the next.

It didn't mean a thing to us. God means hardly a
thing to many of our young people today.

Once upon a time, somebody died and went to
heaven. When he got there he said to God, "Why did
you make me, God?" And God said,
"Because I *wanted* to!"

We are too complicated. We have made God
too complicated. We have been so anxious to define
and to control, that God has been lost in all the
definitions, the rituals and the rules. God is. And
that, perhaps, is too simple for us. In her book *The
Color Purple,* Alice Walker portrays a deeply
beautiful and simple image of God as One who is
constantly trying to attract our attention and wanting
to be loved:

But once us feel loved by God, us do the best we can to please him with what us like. You telling me God love you, and you ain't never done nothing for him? I mean, not go to church, sing in the choir, feed the preacher and all like that?
But if God love me, Celie, I don't have to do all that. Unless I want to. There's a lot of other things I can do that I speck God likes.
Like what? I ast.
Oh, she say. I can lay back and just admire stuff. Be happy. Have a good time.
Well, this sound like blasphemy sure nuff.
She say, Celie, tell the truth, have you ever found God in church? I never did. I just found a bunch of folks hoping for him to show. Any God I ever felt in church I brought in with me. And I think all the other folks did too. They come to church to *share* God, not find God.

THE COLOR PURPLE, ALICE WALKER
WASHINGTON SQUARE PRESS 1982

BREAKFAST ON THE BEACH

We have to create new rituals which are not deadly and do not put our children to sleep and make our old ones nod off. We have to be about the business of ritualizing the sacred in a way that is meaningful and alive to people.

For over twenty years our lay mission communities in the Volunteer Missionary Movement have been creating ritual. Along with thousands of other small Christian communities throughout the world, we have been quietly getting on with the business of working, praying and ritualizing. We've been creating rituals alongside the traditional, male rituals, because people needed to be nourished in new and different, but more meaningful ways.

On one occasion, Easter was coming up and our lay community was going to have a ceremony on Holy Thursday. The bishop has a little house in the grounds of the retreat center where we lived. I was walking in our community garden when I happened to run in to him. I often run into bishops. He was always a little suspicious of what might be going on in our lay mission center, because he saw all these women and men involved in Christian mission, coming and going to and from far away lands, and praying and working together. The bishop often must have wondered, 'What goes on over there? —Are they keeping the rules?'

Anyway, we met in the garden, and the bishop said to me, "What are you going to do for Easter?"

"Well," I said, "We're going to celebrate. We're going to make a big stew on Holy Thursday night with lamb and wild herbs. We are going to put cushions on the floor and sit in the chapel, and we are going to eat the stew with unleavened bread."

"Oh, you're going to sit on the floor eating stew?"

"Yes."

"Um... Are you going to do the washing of the feet?"

"Yes, we are."

"Well, mmm... Could I ask you, Edwina, who's going to wash the feet?"

"I'm going to wash the feet."

"Oh really? You know, Edwina, that's *not* the mind of the church."

"But, bishop, my community has asked me to wash the feet."

"Yes, but that's not the way it should be done, you know."

"This is the way we have chosen to do it."

"Um..." said the bishop, "Could I come along?"

"Of course. You're welcome to join us. I hope you don't mind sitting on the floor."

"No, no. That's fine."

So along comes the bishop and we are all prepared with the dishes and the stew and the bread and everything on the floor in the chapel. There's a wonderful atmosphere, candles are lit, the music is playing. But the bishop is pacing up and down outside the chapel. And I said, "Are you alright, bishop?"

"IT'S NOT THE MIND OF THE CHURCH, my

dear. You know, Edwina, I think –I think *I* should
wash the feet." The poor man was most
uncomfortable. And then suddenly, as if inspired,
he said, "I have a good idea! Why don't I wash and
you dry?" I looked at this man and thought –*he
really needs to do the washing!* This is really
important to him. "Okay. Here's the washcloth. You wash and
I'll dry."

That's alright. We must not create services and
rituals where who does what becomes more important
than the meaning of the act itself. To do so would be
to repeat the problems that have been created for us
by patriarchy, where only certain hierarchical folk
do this and only the bishop does that.

The bishop came and he was happy. He went
around with his bowl, washing all the feet. And the
community was compassionate, because it wasn't a
big deal who washed our feet. What was important
was the whole symbolism of the ritual, and how we
might apply it in our own lives.

Our God is gentle. Our God is compassionate.
Our God is free and will have no dealings with exclusion.
No dealings with power. No dealings with barriers.
As the Maasai women in East Africa sing,
God is warm, moist and salty.
Oh, isn't that so much more colorful and meaningful
than the notion of a God who is Almighty, King,
Lord, Judge and Father! Doesn't it feel more *real* to
have a God who is Warm, Moist and Salty?

The traditional African, Native American, and indeed many nomadic peoples have achieved an understanding of God's nature as being rooted, grounded in creation: a fluid nature encompassing all that is. On the other hand, we of the domineering, supposedly 'advanced' societies tend towards rigid, exclusionary definitions of God. Yet God remains the God of those people who hold her close, as children hold their mother. It is in them that we shall find her, and she will empower us to make a difference.

❦

I have learned a good deal from the prostitutes with whom I work. Often, we middle-class folks who are into church and religion get carried away with our sense of the rather lofty call to reach out to the so-called 'poor' and 'marginalized.' We get a bit stiff and take ourselves ever so seriously. On a number of occasions the women have said to me, "Come on Edwina, loosen up," and suchlike. And then I hear God laughing. Yes, we need to loosen up. We need to remember that the world has been saved already. God is always ahead of us.

Jesus was never into pomp and circumstance. He didn't take himself so seriously that he separated himself from the ordinary folk on the streets. Jesus was rooted in reality. Even after the Resurrection, Jesus maintained his 'earthiness.' In the Gospel of John, Peter and the disciples are feeling glum and let down after the death of Jesus, they have lost their fire, hanging around listlessly. Then Peter, I suspect rather roughly, declared "I'm going fishing."

—Anything to distract from the terrible events surrounding the crucifixion. So off they all went and fished all night long without catching a single trout.

At daybreak they rowed back to the shore. There was someone standing there waving. "How did you do?" He shouted. It was clear from Peter's face how they had done. Then the stranger brightly came out with the maddening suggestion: "Why don't you try the other side of the boat?" He was obviously one of those smart-alec types who turn up at the very end of an unsuccessful working day and offer gratuitous advice. Peter was by then in the mood where he would do anything to show that nothing worked. Life and work and even fishing were meaningless. So for the hell of it, he let down the net to show the guy on shore what an idiot he was.

The nets nearly broke with the weight of the catch. The disciples were awe-struck. It was a miracle. But the man on the beach had gone. Dragging the nets to shore, they saw him kneeling on the sand, he had gathered drift-wood for a fire. He turned and called out, "Bring some fish, I'm frying breakfast!" They knew that he was Jesus. The Risen Lord was making their breakfast on the beach.

As they ate, Jesus challenged Peter: "Do you love me?" Three times he asked the same question. The third time, Jesus responded to Peter's 'Yes,' by saying, "Then feed my people." He demonstrated how it was to be done—without pomp or glory or ceremony God's people are to be fed and nourished. It was not beneath the resurrected, glorified Jesus to kneel in the sand and make a fish-fry for his friends. God is warm, she feeds her people. One way or another, we must do the same.

TELL THEM

Breaking through the powers of darkness
bursting from the stifling tomb
he slipped into the graveyard garden
to smell the blossomed air.

Tell them, Mary, Jesus said,
that I have journeyed far
into the darkest deeps I've been
in nights without a star.

Tell them, Mary, Jesus said,
that fear will flee my light
that though the ground will tremble
and despair will stalk the earth
I hold them firmly by the hand
through terror to new birth.

Tell them, Mary, Jesus said,
the globe and all that's made
is clasped to God's great bosom
they must not be afraid
for though they fall and die, he said,
and the black earth wrap them tight
they will know the warmth
of God's healing hands
in the early morning light.

Tell them, Mary, Jesus said,
smelling the blossomed air,
tell my people to rise with me
to heal the Earth's despair.

Mysticism

In the beginning there was the Spirit of God. Wisdom. Sophia. 'Ruah' in Hebrew. Co-creator with God. In the Hebrew scriptures, she danced and was playful, and called the earth, the world, the cosmos into being. The Spirit, full of energy and imagination, worked side by side as Co-creator with Yahweh, bringing forth and giving birth to the earth. She was the feminine principle. She was female. In the Hebrew scriptures, she plays a significant role under the title Sophia, or Wisdom.

She was a powerful force in the beginning, but today, Sophia, feminine wisdom is little known or understood. We rarely talk of the Holy Spirit as Wisdom and female. Slowly she has been edged out of our traditions. Sophia was marginalized in favor of the single, male Yahweh, because Sophia was too exuberant, too playful and too creative for our rigid Church doctrines. The feminine dimension of God's creative power had to be suppressed in order to maintain rationale and logic in our codes, canons and rituals. And so Sophia was left to the fringe groups, the school of John, the poets, the artists and the mystics, who were always a bit wild and on the edges.

In spite of being marginalized Sophia has never ceased to be a gentle presence in our world. Today Sophia-Wisdom is resurfacing in our consciousness. Little by little, from a deep level, the Spirit of

Wisdom is showing herself, particularly among women. Previously, Sophia had found a home with the mystics, especially the early female mystics.

The mystics are God's last resort. They are dreamers, and they are not paralyzed by rule and doctrine. They have encountered a God who electrifies them, who fills them with an entrancing vision and hope for the human race. Sophia dwells in the hearts of those who seek new dreams and hope for a more wholesome world: the Dorothy Days, the Martin Luther Kings, the Archbishop Romeros... Sophia rejoices in the visionaries and the peace-makers. She fills them. In a world which is hungry, tired and seeking, God's presence is shown in Sophia through people who are open to the mystical.We have to loosen up if we are to experience, in our frightened and insecure world, God's wholesome vision and dream for the human race, born of both the masculine Yahweh and the feminine Sophia.

Mystics break through with a new vision. They say to people, 'Look! There *is* another way, another possibility.' But in their journey, mystics first hit rock-bottom themselves. The experience of mysticism is a salvation experience where the mystic comes to know the aching loneliness and darkness within which God may move in the human heart. Mystics emerge from turmoil. They come out of darkness and break through with God's message: 'I am with you in spite of your darkness and pain.' And they can say this because they have experienced the darkness themselves.

Julian of Norwich was a mystic, an Englishwoman, born in 1342. Interestingly, she was nameless. She took her name from the church she lived in, St. Julian's in the city of Norwich. A nameless woman, as are so many.

Julian wanted to get into the skin of Jesus. She wanted fully to empathize with Jesus to the point that she would experience the pain that he suffered. I think lots of folks go through a period, when they are young and passionate, wanting to identify with a saint or a guru or Jesus. When I was a teenager, I wanted to be like Jesus, I wanted to love like he did and give myself to God. And so, Julian in her passion, in her longing for God, wanted to know the passion of Jesus. And, poor woman, she did! She became so sick, so ill, that she was on the brink of death. It's really not too smart to play games with God. God takes us seriously.

It was in experiencing near death, that she was scooped up by God, who assured her that she would live: God was with her. She came forward from escaping death with a powerful awareness of life and hope: 'Guess what? I nearly died, but I didn't die. But I know what it's like to be in the pits, I know what it's like.' It gave her an astonishing personal knowledge of God-With-Us. The passing on of that knowledge is evangelization.

The experience of conversion must be passed on to the community. Julian moved from the personal piety of 'Me and Jesus, Jesus and I suffering together for the sins of the world,' to the experience of pain and confusion leading to salvation. From this comes conversion. God's message, revealed to Julian was one of hope and comfort for all:

> I will make all things well, I shall make all things well. I may make all things well, and I can make all things well; and you will see that yourself, that all things will be well.
>
> *JULIAN OF NORWICH: SHOWINGS CH.15* †

It is a message we desperately need to hear authentically spoken today.

Julian lived in a time when there was a lot of trouble in England. There had been the Hundred Years War, the Peasant Revolt, and then the great plague known as the Black Death, which wiped out half of Europe. Imagine this virus! –Imagine it without medical technicians, doctors and scientists. No-one knew what was going on. They knew only that their friends, colleagues, relations died within twelve hours of falling ill. One minute they were fine, then they were dead. People couldn't understand what was happening. They were terrified. The only interpretation they could come up with was, 'God's punishing us! We are sinful, we are guilty.' AIDS is a similar tragedy. It is rampant and growing. People are dying. We're trying to stop it, trying to solve it, but people are dying, and they are afraid. Today as in the Middle Ages, people are hungry to understand, to be comforted, to believe that there *is* a loving, compassionate God.

---

† Full attribution of all passages quoted appears in the section *More Reading*, at the end of the book.

Three episodes of the plague visited the people in Julian's lifetime. She survived them all. She came out alive, saying, "It's alright! It's alright! We are brought to our knees, we have to struggle like this, but it's okay, God is still with us."

Julian began to use terms for God such as 'Mother,' 'Mother Comforter.' This woman who had nearly died herself, talked about God in tender, comforting images.

> As truly as God is our Father, so truly is God our Mother... The Second Person, who is our Mother... has now become our Mother sensually.
> *JULIAN OF NORWICH: SHOWINGS CH.58 & 59*

The only reason she could preach to the people and get through to them, was because she knew what she was talking about. She had been on the journey. And so, today, women who have been on the journey of disintegration, of oppression and pain, are the ones who will call forth salvation from the community. They are the ones who will assure us of God's presence. That is where the new life is. The life is where there's been pain and struggling. Anyone who sticks with a twelve-step program will tell you that.

But people of Medieval England, because they couldn't diagnose AIDS or the plague, felt that they were sinful, and therefore guilty. And this was endorsed by the Church. The Catholic Church developed the whole business of Confession around this time. They felt they had to appease a God who was angry and vengeful. The Church, saying, 'We are a guilty people, we are a sinful people, and we must ask forgiveness,' brought into the consciousness of the whole community a sense of fear and guilt.

Original sin came into its own and has been with us ever since. People are basically evil, deserving of punishment. Punishment and guilt have been picked up, particularly by the Catholic Church and used, consciously or unconsciously, to keep bowed down and cowed, what should be a vibrant, alive people, eyes filled with God's life and sparkling with the joy of Sophia. The mystics are not like that. The mystics celebrate and accept the darkness as a way to understand and enjoy salvation and God's light. That is their message.

Julian declared that God is incapable of anger. God is not angry. God is not going to Zap us! God just wants to help us understand Wisdom, and what Wisdom is all about. God, said Julian, never promised that we would not suffer. Furthermore, her vision enabled her to say that we will not be overcome. God did *not* say we would not be troubled or disquieted. And that's the message of hope.

God showed Julian that the human race has two major problems, impediments to wholeness. One is that we are impatient with our pains and our burdens. We can't deal with pain, we can't deal with burdens. Our society is continually saying, 'Oh, we must get rid of all pain, we must get rid of all suffering. Don't suffer, don't go through pain. On television we are assailed by advertisements that would have us believe we are about to be struck down by all manner of pains and diseases and that we must arm ourselves with a host of pills, potions and medicines to allay any discomfort. The message is clear and constant: If you're not suffering now, guess what? –Tomorrow you'll get arthritis, hemorrhoids, or whatever. Pain must be avoided at all costs, it must not be allowed into our reality. On all levels, we're trying to numb people against darkness and pain.

But on the spiritual journey it is vital. It is vital we come to understand that in spite of the reality of darkness in our world, there is also God's presence, God's light and God's grace. We will not be whole until we learn to face, embrace and integrate that shadow and darkness, with God's light and God's grace.

The second thing that God revealed to Julian as a stumbling-block to the human race is despair. We give up too easily. We have such a tiny, tiny light of faith. Despair destroys hope. The Spirit of Wisdom, the Spirit of Light, the Spirit of Sophia breaks through in the darkness and says, 'There *is* hope, there is light in all the darkness.'

Women especially, need to be aware of that. Something sucks us down, and would have us despair if the light is not kept in us. We will hit rock bottom. As individuals, we must not try to escape that journey into ourselves, the journey of pain, of acknowledging the world's sin, yes, old-fashioned 'sin.' Not only must we individually hit rock bottom, but also as a *people*. As a people, as a nation, as a country, we *will* be bowed down. We will be bowed down so that we might experience salvation.

The journey that belongs to us as individuals, also belongs to us as a people and in the end it must be experienced as a people. When that time comes, and when we as a people are brought down, unable to control our pain, the light of faith that is left, the Spirit of Sophia that is in the community will say: 'It's okay. We will raise ourselves up, because God is with us.' Truly then, we will be a people of God, transformed.

As each individual is transformed on this journey of conversion, so the community must experience this journey of conversion. The mystics try to tell us that. We must follow a very similar path to that of the mystics. And all will be well if we are faithful to that journey.

> Heal the broken
> With comforting words of God,
> Cheer them gently
> With earthly joys.
> Be merry and laugh
> With the broken
> And carry their secret needs
> In the deepest silence of your heart.

MEDITATIONS WITH MECHTILD OF MAGDEBURG

Mrs. Murphy at the Divine Olympics

Some years ago, a Chicago newspaper featured an article in which they described me as 'a devout Catholic with the tongue of a pagan tart.' Now, I don't know what they meant by 'devout Catholic' I suspect there are different interpretations on that score. 'Pagan tart' –well, in England, a tart is a little pastry with a bit of jelly in the middle. No-one ever described me as a little pastry before...

I've reflected on that description, and I thought: "How have I changed in these years?" When I was growing up, I really *did* want to do everything right. I wanted to listen, to learn and to grow. And I was, indeed, a devout Catholic in that I went to Mass, not only every Sunday, but every day. I went to confession every Saturday afternoon, Benediction every Sunday evening. I joined the Legion of Mary. I was also in the Sodality of Our Lady, and in the church choir. I embraced *everything!* I said, "Yes, yes, yes. Teach me. Tell me. I will do it all." When I joined the Sodality, I knew I could wear a veil, just like Our Lady. And, I could be in the church procession for the May Queen, and I could do all those things, and they became very important to me. Yes, I was a devout Catholic.

And then I went to Africa. And I discovered that it wasn't like what they had said. When I went to Africa I took my God with me, my white, male, Catholic, British God. I wanted to tell the African people all about the one true God and the one true

Church. But, the biggest shock I ever had in my life was that God had got to Africa before me! God was already there, present in the lives and rituals of these 'poor' African tribes, present in their banana plantations, their mud huts, their hospitality, their warmth. I discovered that God was much BIGGER than the white, Catholic Englishman God I knew. Africa changed and stretched me, and helped me understand that God grows with us as we grow in experience and understanding. If we are open to the journey, God 'becomes' all the time.

I was disturbed because I had faithfully gathered all the traditions, all the ways, and loved them and made them mine. And then things began to shift and change. It was the African people who introduced me to a new way, a different way of looking at reality. The shift that I was beginning to experience was not very comfortable.

Once upon a time, there was a little girl called Mary. As she grew from infancy, she started walking on her hands instead of her feet. Her parents saw this, and they were distraught because clearly the child wasn't normal, she wasn't developing in the right way. So they called in the psychologist, and they called in the therapist and the teachers and the counselors, and they worked and worked on the child, and eventually they turned her over! They turned her up the *right* way. And little Mary began to walk on her feet, just like everybody else. Her parents said to her, "Isn't it wonderful? Now you're like us, now you're like everybody. Now you can see the same way that we all can see!" And the child said, "No, no. Because, you see, when I was walking on my hands, I ran eyeball to eyeball into a butterfly, and a worm sat on my nose."

Little Mary knew that she would never see the world in quite the same way, now that she had been flipped over to the normal position. Whilst she walked upside down, she had a different and unique perspective on the world.

That is what is happening. Many of us, particularly women, are beginning, so to speak, to walk on our hands. We're beginning to see the world from a different perspective, and we're saying, "Oh! This never happened to me before!" We are beginning to voice thoughts and ask questions that we never dared.

The shift is dangerous, and the shift makes us a little nervous. Much that we have been taught about God and our traditions no longer fits our contemporary experience. We were taught that God is far away from us, so far away that we have to go through all kinds of prescribed benedictions and rituals and ways of worshipping and words and readings and retreats, in order to reach God, for whom we all long.

It is as if we have made up a God who comes packaged with a Divine Olympics. This God who burst us forth, we have made into the One who says, "I love you and I have burst you forth, but if you want to get to know me, you've got to jump through this hoop, you've got to tunnel through here, you've got to climb these steps..." And we have to go through all these obstacles —ladders to the Divine. We have separated ourselves from God, and put between us all these steps and difficulties, so the people of God begin to say, "I can never touch the divine. I can never reach the holy. I am far away, alienated." That's how most folks feel –out of touch with their inherent divinity.

There are no spiritual Olympics, there is no divine treasure-hunt, except that we invented them. We invented them. Maybe subconsciously, we felt the need to control and mediate people's journeys to God and their understanding of the holy. When people feel that they are unworthy of, or unable to touch the divine, there are those amongst us who are ready to mediate between the poor 'laity' and the holy. Here is the chance to wield tremendous power and control over the ordinary people of this world, the Mrs. Murphys who knock at the rectory door looking for God. The treasure-hunt, the path to the divine is manned by legions of intermediaries who stand between God and Mrs. Murphy, to tell her what's going on in her life, with or without God.

It is not that spiritual guidance and direction is irrelevant. No, it can be very important, having special and meaningful purpose at certain stages of our journeys. The point I am trying to make is that millions of God's people feel alienated from a God they have never been encouraged to recognize as living within *themselves,* a God accessible to everyone.

In his book, *Song of the Bird* Anthony De Mello tells the story of a man riding fast through town on a donkey. Everybody asked "What are you doing? What's the big rush?" The man yelled back over his shoulder,
"I'm looking for my donkey!"
We are all like that. God is intimately involved in

the everyday fibre of our lives and being, yet we are *always looking for God*. And we have been taught that if we are even remotely to approach God, the journey is one long struggle, the great haul, and we need to read and study and know a lot. Many of us give up, saying, 'We are not worthy, we cannot do those things, we are far away from the sacred. We haven't the money to go off on retreat or the time to spend in hermitages. So, we'll never get to be anywhere near holy. How can we when we're stuck with a job, a family and a mortgage?'

It has always struck me as being not quite right that only a chosen few have the luxury of retreats, spiritual guidance, theology studies, etc. Does it really mean that poor old Mrs. Murphy is left out of the spiritual journey? Does it mean that the journey is to be left to the traditional 'religious,' the monks, the nuns and priests, and those who have time and money to spend on God-knowledge and God-journeying? It doesn't seem to be the way God would order things.

Some time ago, I was invited to give a Day on Prayer to some religious sisters. As the day drew closer, I began to reflect: "How can *I* stand in front of all those sisters and talk about God and prayer?" And the more I thought about it, the more uneasy I became. I felt I couldn't communicate God to all these women who had been on retreat, and who had read all the books and the theology and that kind of thing. What did I have to say? What did I, an ordinary laywoman, have to say about prayer, the holy, – God? Suddenly, I felt very insecure and inadequate to the task. And then I had a brainwave!

I would collect my slides of Africa, pictures of the sunsets, the mountains, the lakes and the rivers. I would gather these, get some classical music, and I'd make an *audiovisual!* I would play it and show it and say to the group, Listen to the music and see the beauty of God's creation –and I'd sit down! I would be off the hook for a good while, with the machine doing my communicating for me. Thinking all this, I was greatly relieved.

I gathered up my tapes and slides, and off I went to the conference, feeling a lot better. They were sitting there, waiting, a hundred sisters. And I got my tapes ready, fine, no problem, I was confident. I took my slides out and checked them, and suddenly I realized I had brought the wrong set! And I heard God laughing.

It was as if the carpet was pulled right from under my feet. And I was left with nothing. My slides, my tapes, everything I had, was hopelessly irrelevant. And there they were, 'Tell us about The Holy.' All I was left with was God and my little bit of faith. I had no choice but to tap into it, to share it. And when there were no more props, no more supports, the God within me was free. I spoke, and I shared my God.

We have *within us* everything that is necessary for transformation, everything that is required for fullness of life. The problem is that our training and our conditioning tells us we cannot become holy, nor approach the holy, without all the intermediaries pleading our cause, and mediating the holy for us.

Was it always like this? Were we always so limited? Were we always so insecure? Are we trying to control so much that we ourselves have no freedom? Most of us have been told, one way or another: 'This is the way it is, we will give you the rules, we will tell you about the divine and the holy, and in order to make it, you must follow all this in the right way.'

What we need to do is free ourselves of much that has given us security. We have to clear the paths before us, strewn with insecurities and doubts, to allow ourselves to expand in God's universe, and believe in our individual, unique potential. We need to get a different perspective. If we look at the development of the cosmos, we see that it has been evolving for fifteen billion years, and we little two-legged humans have shown up at the party at just the last minute. In cosmic terms, we have only begun to evolve and to grow. But we say, 'Here we are, it's our party now. We are in control, we understand everything, we've got it all together!' We are blissfully unaware that in reality, the cosmos, God's Word, God's creation has been humming along nicely for all those billions of years without us!

What we have lost, in this arrogant defining of God, the holy, even human destiny, is an awe, a wonderment that comes from the realization that we are not in control, but God is. And our lives are a continuous unfolding of God's presence in the world and within us. We simply cannot predict the process of God's unfolding.

MADE HOLY

We are made holy
by our recognition
of God in us.

God is in all and everything.
But the reality of
God's presence
only comes about
through human recognition.
Ah then!
We have the power
to sacrilize the world.

VIRGIN, MOTHER, CRONE

Once, some scientists did an experiment. They took a jar and put some insects in it. Bzzz... Imagine a bunch of insects in the jar. They put the lid on the jar, screwed it down, and let it sit there with the insects buzzing inside. And as the insects buzzed and buzzed, instinctively they were aware of their boundaries –they had some sense of their space within the jar. Then one day the scientists came along and took the lid off the jar. And the insects buzzed and buzzed around. But even though the lid was off, they stayed in the jar, because they were fixed in that reality. That was the way it was. They couldn't imagine that there was any other way of being. Their entire existence had been controlled and monitored for them, to the point that there was no escape into the new possibilities outside the jar.

We are like that, buzzing around in our own little realities saying, "This is it, this is it." We have closed off the incredible revelation of God and the universe. We even closed the Canon of Scripture— the written revelation of God-with-Us. God's revelation ended with Jesus of Nazareth, and we of the twentieth century look back to the experience of the Hebrew people and to Jesus as the final word. How could we? How could we do that in the context of God's enormous fertility and very BIGNESS? How *could* we say, 'That's it folks!' Though God continues to reveal God-self, we have not been trained to see the signs nor intuit God's continuing presence. We put the lid on the jar and said, "That's it!"

But God is bursting out. Revelation is not over. The book is not closed –not in truth. The lid is off the jar, we must now get out of it and say, "God is bigger than this." As we break down the old system, and as it becomes clear that the lid is off, some of us are beginning to buzz out and to fly. And some folks are saying, "Wow!"

But then some are returning to the jar, because out there, in the great beyond, things are big and scary. Suddenly, everything that was familiar and comfortably secure is gone. Even within themselves, some are now wondering who they really are, whereas before, in the jar, safe and secure, they entertained no such ridiculous question. But now, suddenly, SZZUMPH! –Ah! The shift is dangerous and uncomfortable, and it is happening inside us, behind our belly-buttons.

It's coming! Along with it comes painful death: the death of the Sodality of Our Lady, the death of plenary indulgences, the death of transubstantiation, of Purgatory, of Confession, of some of our rituals and our concretely held doctrines and beliefs, the death of a god made only in our own image and likeness and according to our limited understanding and perceptions

Now there is another space, bigger and darker and deeper. This does not mean that the traditions and ways of childhood and young adulthood have been unimportant. These traditions have been a necessary and beautiful part of the journey and growth. But once upon a time we were fed with milk and now we must eat meat. Once upon a time we were children, and now we are adults. And maybe we will be taken where we would not choose to go. But maybe now, we will look on Revelation as something that is with God's people —all of them, all of the time. We need to learn to recognize the presence of a God who is beyond our definitions.

It is important to keep our fifteen-billion-year development in perspective, to realize how slowly and gradually we are evolving in God's universe. It is important to recognize that there have been many different kinds of society and people who have worshipped God in different ways before us.

Five thousand years ago, things were a little different. In those days, Revelation was not closed. People worshipped God as they experienced God's presence in nature, in their daily lives and in their communities. God was an integral part of society. This was the time when there was peace on Earth and society lived in harmony. This was the time when giving birth and rearing children were the most important functions of civilization. God was female —a concept alien to a people raised on a Father God. God was perceived as feminine, the one who gave birth to humanity, because as a woman, she was capable of giving birth.

There was a time when God was honored as Mother, and peace, arts, crafts, childbirth, nurturing were what humanity held as central to life. There was a trinitarian symbol for God of three connecting circles. This was the holy symbol of these people who lived five thousand years and more ago, in a society which worshipped God as feminine. In the representation of the circles, God, the holy was shown as Virgin, Mother and Crone; very different from Father, Son and Spirit.

Father, Son and Spirit: Virgin, Mother and Crone. One the masculine way, one the feminine. Birth, represented by the Virgin, was extremely important in that ancient civilization, it was seen as a great mystery, a divine event to be honored and revered. Birth was central. Because this neolithic society honored the power and mystery of childbirth, there was peace and nurturing, not violence and devastation. There was caring instead of competition. Theirs was the only time that we know when there was not war on Earth. Life was represented by the circular symbol for Mother, and Death by the third spiral, the Crone, the one who journeyed into darkness.

Ironically, the sacred symbol for these peace-loving people of five-thousand years ago, was the serpent. The serpent was a sign of wisdom and a symbol of knowledge. But eventually, this nurturing, mother and goddess-centered civilization disintegrated with the invasions of the Indo-European horsemen, who brought with them a god who was male, a warrior and conqueror. With these invasions came a new set of values: competition, land ownership, conquest, weaponry. The civilization which honored the Mother Goddess gradually succumbed to a male-oriented society whose God was the Warrior King.†

In the Mother Goddess era, the power of menstruation was very strong. Woman's blood, woman's menstrual period was a holy period because it was part of the mystery of childbirth. Men could not understand how women were able to produce

---

† There are many erudite accounts of this momentous period. Robert Graves, in the introduction to his *The Greek Myths,* Penguin Books 1955, writes: 'Ancient Europe had no gods. The Great Goddess was regarded as immortal, changeless and omnipotent, and the concept of fatherhood had not been introduced into religious thought.'

life, but they were aware that women's ability to give birth was connected with the mystery of menstrual blood. Then when men became warriors with weapons, they too were able to shed blood, though in a different way. The ability to shed blood through violence became a sign of male power which eventually overshadowed the female power symbolized by menstruation.

So, there was an historical shift to a new reality. God became warrior, male, king, Yahweh who rules over all peoples. The feminine, the birthing, the process, the holiness of the Earth and all that brings about new life and new birth, was lost to the drive for power and conquest. Later on, much of what was revered by the society of the Mother Goddess, the sacredness of the Earth, the holiness of motherhood, the joy of new life, would re-emerge in the mystics.

In order to facilitate the change from the Mother Goddess society to the Father God society, there had to be some radical changes in myth and symbol. The serpent, the symbol of God as Mother, had to be repressed or co-opted. We can see the degree to which the co-opting succeeded when we look at the modern statue of the Virgin Mary crushing the serpent beneath her feet. (I always wondered what Mary was doing standing on a serpent). In order to destroy all remnants of a time when humanity behaved differently, when there was a partnership society, with men and women working and living as equals, the serpent had to be annihilated. What better way to do it than to take Mary, the Virgin Mother, and have the woman herself destroy the serpent, the symbol of her own power. And what better way to do it than to have the serpent seduce Eve, who would be made responsible for the Fall of humanity? It was inevitable that Eve, as a woman, would look to the serpent, her symbol for wisdom, for all-knowledge. The myth was so reconstituted that the serpent, All Wisdom, became the serpent, All Evil. Women have never recovered.

We have to look at these kinds of things. We have to be aware that our society is unbalanced and that somewhere along the line there has been some deception. If we look at the Virgin, Mother and Crone, we see that the Church has selected some of the symbolism and used it to full (male) advantage. Virginity, for instance, was held up as the ideal state for the perfect woman. The Virgin Mary replaced the notion of a fertile Mother Goddess, and the ancient concept of woman-power as manifested in childbirth was lost to the new ideal of virginity. To be a mother became second best to being a virgin, and gradually, throughout the ages, Mother also lost its ancient and awesome meaning and was reduced to the kind of apple-pie, cheery-mom image we often associate with Hallmark cards on Mother's Day. The power and status of women was successfully, relentlessly eroded.

The Crone was the problem. The Crone represented the Age of Wisdom (Sophia-Spirit). The Crone is a woman grown, gray-haired and wise. The Crone is the wise woman. She's the dangerous one. She is the one who may begin to ask the important and difficult questions in her later life, challenging the community. In ancient history, the Crone was the one to whom people went for understanding, wisdom and advice. She was familiar with the underworld, the dark journey into self and life and, ultimately, death. She was, without doubt, the hardest symbol of the ancient ways to co-opt or destroy. But eventually it was done. She was made the object of scorn and rejection, one who was no longer of use to society. And if you look at our society today, any notion of respect for the Crone is eliminated. Old women? Put them in a nursing home. Old women? They are useless, they have nothing to say. There is no room in our society for the old woman. The once revered Crone is now the old hag. Ironically, the word 'hag' now used in derision and abuse, once meant 'holy.'

The holy woman of the people who lived in the time of the partnership society when God was female, has been successfully reduced to a nobody. The one who once carried within her the wisdom of the community and who was a source of knowledge in ancient times, and in many tribal civilizations, is seen as having nothing to offer our society. The process of reducing the wisdom represented by the female Elder is repeated in many tribal cultures, where such wisdom is today no longer taken into account. We have successfully 'evangelized.'

Another distortion of the role and meaning of the Crone came in her being condemned as a witch, often described as the 'Old Witch,' seen in many of our fairy tales as a symbol of evil. But the Anglo-Saxon word for witch, 'wicce' or 'wycke' is related to the words 'wit' and 'wis.' She is more sage than sorceress.

In the Middle Ages, it was in fact the witches who practised some of those ancient ways of the Mother Goddess period. They were familiar with the medicinal properties of herbs, with the cycles of the moon and the power of gems. They were the healers, the midwives who helped ease the pain of women in labor. These were the descendants and followers of the Crone.

And, of course, we know of the witch-hunts of medieval and later centuries, where millions of women were burnt and butchered, because these midwives-witches-crones too dangerously recalled the ancient ways of the Mother of five thousand and more years ago. Deep in our subconscious, or male subconscious, lurked the terror that the feminine was re-emerging in the wise women, the elders, the witches. Between nine and thirteen million women, and some men who supported them, were slaughtered in the attempt to eradicate the resurfacing memory of the Great Mother.

But the Crone, the one who knows about darkness and death, the one who is familiar with the ways of the underworld, will not be totally repressed. She is now re-emerging. And now she cannot be burned. But our society, still fearing the feminine, tries other, more subtle ways to repress the new consciousness which is arising in woman.

Our task is enormous: to co-create with God. To look at all that has gone before us, and to recognize that each one of us, however small, has a unique task in co-creation—a unique contribution to make in the world and to humanity—to recognize that by our very existence, we are related to all things; to the caterpillar, the sod, the animals, the birds, to every man and woman. We are related to the children, the stars, the plants, flowers and foliage. We are part of an interconnected, interrelated cosmos. We cannot amputate ourselves from the rest of God's unfolding universe. We must come to discover the part we have to play in it.

What does the holy say to me? What does the Hag say? What does Wycke say? What does Wisdom say in my belly-button? What part do I have to play in the development of the cosmos? And, where is this Spirit, wandering free today, saying, "Come out of the jar and fly?"

FEMININE WISDOM

She rose from the shadows,
ancient, magnificent,
cloaked in soft brown wool
that smelt of moist earth,
her eyes shone deep wet
reflecting the wisdom
of ages past, and present,
and yet to come.
She held a rounded stone
which shone like crystal
and a yellow black serpent
hugged her sapped bosom.
Ah, she rose from the shadows
of ancient history
into the consciousness
of millions of souls seeking
wholeness, harmony and hope,
longing for the wisdom
of the great sleeping mother.
She rose from the shadows,
ancient, magnificent,
and the belly of the ocean
stirred as humanity
groaned in her birthing.

ROTTEN, HORRIBLE PEOPLE

People are hungry because all is not well. People are frightened, insecure, lonely, homeless. People are looking for the way. They are hungry for the feminine, they are hungry for healing, they are hungry for the Earth in its fullness, they are hungry for God. There is an acute spiritual starvation in our world. The spiritual starvation which people experience is, I believe, compounded by the guilt we have accepted, going all the way back to Eve and the seduction by the serpent. We can see this effect in our rituals.

For example, we can take the Roman Catholic Eucharistic celebration. The people come to gather at Mass on Sunday with hope in their eyes, looking for meaning and comfort. They come to God's holy place looking for food –bread, and words of joy and kindness. But once in the church, God's holy place, rarely do the people's eyes sparkle. They seldom appear relaxed and joyful at being in the home of their Mother, their Father, their God. Among the first words the hungry people hear are:

Let us pause for a moment and remember our sins.

—*Why?* Haven't we suffered enough? Are we not beaten down enough? What is wrong with us that we have to go into God's holy place and think about our sins? Are not our sins ever before us, everywhere we look in our world?

Let us imagine, at Thanksgiving, a mother calling her children to come home to celebrate. She is going to gather all her children and grandchildren and have a big Thanksgiving dinner! She is planning a banquet. And all her children, with their children, gather round the parents' house for Thanksgiving dinner. Can you imagine the joy of the mother inviting her children to the feast, all hungry, expectant, and gathered round the table?

Then, just before they're about to dive into the food, mother says... "Hang on there. Stop a moment! Don't carve that turkey! Before we eat this turkey, I want all of you to remember all the rotten, horrible things you did last week!" –I mean, be real. Does a mother do that? And suddenly the faces of the children and the grandchildren fall.

"O God, you know, I'm such a rotten, horrible person. I was so angry last week, I was impossible..." Do you think they are going to enjoy that turkey?

All too often we have presented our children with a God who says: "I love you with an everlasting love. But, in actual fact, when I think about it, you are not worthy of the great love I have for you, you miserable little worm!" Do you know what we are producing? Christian schizophrenes.

"God loves me, God loves me not. Yes God does, Oh no God doesn't! Oh, I am such a miserable, awful person!" No wonder God's people are paralyzed! No wonder, God scratches her head and says,

"What did you do? What did you do to my children? You know I love them. How *dare* you put them in a jar and make them feel 'Buzzz... We are miserable, guilty sinners.' How dare you not allow them to enjoy my banquet!"

Any psychologist would question this internal contradiction and recognize the damage it can do. Any therapist understands that if you say to children, or to adults, for that matter, "You're not worthy of my love, but I love you anyway," you are going to confuse them, make them feel insecure. Neither adults nor children who are conditioned in this way are going to dance in joy and love. Yet we have made these guilt-trips an essential part of our worship and our ritual. They are remnants of the age-old conspiracy to keep people down and not allow them to think that God could grow within them.

Surely our task in the world is hard enough without making our worship guilt-ridden, fraught with the unspoken, but insistent reminder that Woman is responsible for all the sin.

After all, she gave the apple to Adam, didn't she?

The guilt of the so-called Fall of the human race is a burden which women today are still carrying, psychologically, emotionally and spiritually. I believe the deep sense of guilt generated by this 'Fall' is also largely responsible for the destructive imbalance between male and female in our society. The systematic exclusion of the feminine has not been accidental. It has left us with an all-male, father, white god, and a model family comprised of a virgin mother, a celibate father and a divine child.

Try it! Model family! We bought it. But this can't *possibly* be a model family! In buying it, we alienated ourselves from the divine potential saying, 'We are not models. We are stunted. We are guilty and we'll never be anything else.'

It is more comfortable to sit in our limited little space, than it is to fly. Because when we fly we take responsibility for our lives, we claim responsibility for Wisdom within, and for pursuing that Wisdom, continuing and participating in the journey of revelation.

The Image and Likeness of God

What happened to man and woman in the image and likeness of God? What happened to woman and man as the temples of the Holy Spirit? Is there a relationship between the distorted vision we have of spirituality, and the pain of the world? I see links in the extreme example of women in prostitution who experience themselves as 'the scum of the earth' and as 'shit.' I must respond with a different vision: "No. You are temples of the Holy Spirit. You are God's works of art." But then, are we who are not in prostitution, all that different?

We may not stand up and say, "We are the scum of the earth." We may just say, "I don't really think I can...Oh, I'm not able...I could never be like..." And so on. We speak in modulated terms, in more subtle ways. But basically, if we are to be involved fully in redemption, we have to take seriously what we read in scriptures:

I have made you to become as Gods.

We *have* to become the image and likeness of God. That is the journey to holiness. But we are retarded with our inheritance, which we must begin to let go, whatever the cost. Meister Eckhart said,

God is at home. It is we who have gone out for a walk.

God is at home within us.

I wonder what would have happened if Jesus had been a battered baby? If, in the womb, Jesus had felt anger or violence from his mother, or was unwanted? And if, when he had been born, Jesus had been battered and raped, would he have grown up believing he was the Son of God? Is it possible that a battered baby could grow up into a sense of self as being the Son, the Daughter of God? And do you think if we treated everybody as if they were Daughters and Sons of God, our world might be different? Mary and Joseph treated Jesus with real love and awe. Even as she carried him in the womb, Mary felt and believed she carried someone holy. Jesus was born into a family which nourished the holy, the divine. And the child grew up as the Son of God.

All of us are called into that process. But we are part of such a history of rape and of battery and psychological violence, that now many children are being born with some defect, fear or inadequacy. We need a healing society to gradually bring this people back to knowing who they are —the Daughters and Sons of God.

When we close off Jesus as the last revelation of God, we close off our own potential. When I was in theology school, I was thinking about this, and I said to my teacher, "You know, if Jesus indeed was, as I believe, the Son of God, could there not be other sons and daughters of God as we grow in faith and wisdom?"

"(Gasp) NO," my teacher breathed. "There is no one who could ever be like the Son of God, who is Jesus."

"Wasn't Jesus the first one, the one who represented the way it was to be for all men and all women, to show us that we too, could be just like

him, and in fact we could do more than Jesus?"
(GASP!) –I continued. "But Jesus said, 'Greater
things than this you will do.' Greater things."
"No, no, no. That belongs to Jesus."
I was made to feel like a heretic. But it made sense
to me. Isn't that what it's all about? Aren't we on a
journey of discovery and becoming? We have ceased
to believe (if we ever did) that we can move
mountains and walk on water. We mouth these
things, stupidly we mouth them. Well, let's stop it!
If we don't believe it, then let's stop saying it and
singing it. At least let us be authentic in our
blindness!

Probably, it's too dangerous for us to believe
that we can be Daughters and Sons of God, and that
we can move mountains and walk on water. The
implications of that, for patriarchy, hierarchy, and
the ones who mediate the holy for us, would be
devastating. It would mean that the hierarchs would
be out of a job. It means that there would be no one
over you to say, "My child, you mustn't do that. Let
me tell you what to do and how to do it." It means
that the locus of spiritual power would be moved
from the hierarchy and the institution into the
individual and the community. It means that we
would have a whole new process, a circular way of
being, where we would sink deep into our own inner
reality instead of forever looking for signs outside
ourselves. Ah! We must fly out of the jar. God is
free and totally, utterly, ridiculously loving. Loving.
Is it too frightening for us to realize how much
freedom God has given us?

A WARM, MOIST, SALTY GOD

Deep in the forest
I found my God
leaping through the trees,
spinning with the glancing sunlight,
caressing with the breeze.
There where the grasses
rose and fell
fanning the perfumed air,
I smelt her beauty,
elusive, free,
dancing everywhere.

Deep in the city
I found my God
weeping in the bar,
prowling beneath the glaring lights,
dodging speeding car.
There where the women
were pimped and raped,
cursing for a light,
I felt her presence,
fierce, deep,
sobbing in the night.

Deep in myself
I found my God
stirring in my guts,
quickening my middle-aged bones,
stilling all my buts.
There where my spirit
had slumbered long,
numbed into a trance,
A moist, warm, salty God
arose,
and beckoned me to Dance.

Running and Dancing and Looking Beautiful

In the scriptures we read the story of the Prodigal Son. It's about this guy who has two sons. And one son says, "I've had enough, I'm going to cash in all the stocks and shares, and I want to sell the car, and I'm going to push off and take a trip to Europe." He wants to have a good time. He's not going to university or college, he just wants to do his own thing. And the father says,

"Don't do that. Stay here with me."

But the boy goes off and does his own thing. And the father waits. And he waits, and he waits. And he watches and he watches. One day, over the hill, he sees his boy coming back home, bowed down. The boy has entered darkness. He is beaten. And the father throws off his coat and *runs* to his son.

In the Gospel, the implication is quite something, because elders in that time and culture didn't even jog or trot, let alone run! Elders walked very slowly, as they do in many tribal cultures. Age is revered. It would be most inappropriate and frowned upon for an elder to run. It's a sign of adolescence. A wise person stands, and it is the young who come and bow and offer honor and respect. For the father to abandon the sign of authority and to run like a youngster to his own son, was outrageous behavior.

God's love and compassion is ridiculous! God is always waiting for us. And the moment we pop our heads out of the jar and cry, "Help!" God throws off her cloak and comes running.

The God of the patriarchy—Father, King, Lord Judge—does not run. This God sits in judgment over a sinful people. But the God of Jesus runs, the God of Jesus weeps. And the God of Jesus throws off power and authority in favor of an embrace: 'Come home, come home.' God is utterly, totally forgiving.

One of the mystics, Mechtild of Magdeburg, said back in the thirteenth century,

> God is like a great Mother, who bends and takes the child from the floor to her bosom.
>
> MEDITATIONS WITH MECHTILD OF MAGDEBURG

This is the feminine image of God. Our children are hungry for a mothering, caring, forgiving God.

Mechtild of Magdeburg had a vision in which God suggested words to this effect: 'I am like the great physician. I am like a great doctor. I go around with medicines and ointments for my people's bruises.' Can you imagine God going around with a medical kit? 'I want to heal you. It'll be okay, just relax and believe that it will be okay,' says this God. 'I will heal my people.' Mechtild continued expressing the vision: *I, God, am your playmate! I will dance and play with you.*

This God whom we have consigned to some great throne far away, is *bored*. This God, this Co-creator, this great Spirit of Sophia is bored because we will no longer play, we will no longer dance. We have so many problems, and we are dealing with so much guilt and pain. And God says, "Who will dance with me? Who will loosen up, who will dance with me?" The Spirit of Sophia, nevertheless, is alive and well and, I think, hovering over the jar, ready to seduce us into new life.

Hildegaard of Bingen was a prophetic woman who looked out over the rim of the jar. She was born almost 900 years ago. Hildegaard was a Benedictine nun, abbess, doctor, theologian, wycke, witch, healer and midwife. She was a woman who embraced at a deep level, many of the ancient arts of the Crone. She believed in the power of the moon, in the healing power of gems, and even before science knew much of anatomy, Hildegaard was able accurately to describe the functions of the liver and to prescribe effective medicines. She wrote a book on medicine and the healing arts, to which some European surgeons still refer.

One wonders where she got all this knowledge. She got it from her belly, her intuitive, instinctive, feminine wisdom. When we grow and develop, and are in tune with the universe, and in tune with God, when we realize that though we are a small part of creation, yet God endows us with *all,* I think we are capable of tapping into our God-given wisdom and instinct. But our heads tell us, "You don't know anything." The free person, filled with the Spirit of Wisdom, can achieve a great deal more than ever can be imagined.

Hildegaard's main thrust was Church reform. She saw the Church as corrupt, and she had no time for the power and authority of Rome, or male dominance. In refusing to accept the authority of a male abbot over her nuns, Hildegaard, nine hundred years ago said "No" to something many religious women are still struggling with, but accepting in the twentieth century! She said, "No. We women can look out for ourselves. We don't need a man to tell us what to do. We have a different way." And she got into trouble for that.

At that time, her nuns were living in a monastery which was overseen by a male abbot, whose community of monks lived in the other half of the building. Rather than live under his authority, Hildegaard said, "We're going. Come on ladies! If this man wants to tell us what to do, we're off!" And they moved. The whole lot of them packed their bags and moved across the river, taking their dowries with them. There they built their own place and took charge of their own lives.

Hildegaard loved clothes. She would have been a great shopper today. She would have been one of those women who have bumper-stickers reading: 'Shop till you drop.' She organized all her nuns into designing their own individual headgear. And she loved jewelry, which she encouraged her sisters to wear, because she believed that external appearances were a sign of inner glory. Dressing, and looking beautiful was a reflection of the beauty within. This was not the mind of the institutional Church! Throughout the history of religious life, the Church has committed itself to de-sexing and de-feminizing nuns. We know all about that. Many nuns today carry all sorts of deep wounds resulting from rules, regulations and lifestyles that were psychologically and emotionally destructive. I don't think God ever wanted that for any of us. Remember God had said to Mechtild, "Dance! I want you to dance! I want you to dance like a royal bride." But we accepted the whole business: that to embrace a life with God, women must de-feminize themselves. I don't think God ever wanted that. God made us to be beautiful and to see ourselves as beautiful.

And that's the problem. Go back to the example of the women in prostitution saying and believing, "We're shit, we're scum, we're nothing!" And there is God saying, "Look what I have made. I love you! You are beautiful!" Hildegaard picked up some of this thinking and feeling, and said, "We are beautiful, and we must dress beautifully." The purpose of the feminine, said Hildegaard, is to manifest God to the world! Because woman gives birth to God constantly.

She also knew that the Earth is our workshop, that we must tend and care for the Earth because if we do not and if we let the Earth go to waste or worse, destroy it, we destroy ourselves. Hildegaard was committed to believing in the interrelationship of all the living things in the cosmos.

To this extraordinary woman, sin is 'drying up.' Sin is when the dancing stops. It is the inability to celebrate. She was a passionate person. But like all mystics, she had no need of an intermediary between her and God. That's why the mystics are so threatening. That's why the Saints, until they are dead, are threatening. They do not require an intermediary because they experience God intimately, and they are ecstatic about it. That's dangerous. As long as there are only a few of them around, the Church will survive as it is. As long as there are not too many people who stumble into the vision of God, the institution will survive and continue to control. As long as there are not too many flying out of the jar, the system will continue.

Who? What, would Hildegaard of Bingen be today? I guess she would be either in a psychiatric facility, or in a prison. We would lock her up. She likely would be excommunicated. But she would not be in the jar, that's for sure. The mystics invite us to loosen up and dance. They invite us to hear, as Mechtild of Magdeburg said, that God is sick with love, burning with desire. The God of the mystics, like the God of the Maasai tribe in East Africa, is definitely moist, warm, and salty. Definitely different. Definitely threatening. Definitely challenging. Definitely female. Definitely male.

It is not that we are now to have a church and a society run by women alone —that would be as unhealthy and unbalanced as what we have now. The early Mother-Goddess society, for all its peacefulness and nurturing, lacked many of what are usually considered healthy 'masculine' qualities and instincts (though they also belong to the female) —planning, discovery, order, rationale, technology, etcetera. It was necessary for human development that the powerful female-centered society should give way to the masculine, achieving a progressive synthesis. The trouble is, the balance has tipped too far, the masculine has all but obliterated the feminine in many instances, and we are now hurtling towards all sorts of disasters and destruction, like an out-of-control adolescent. The imbalance of the male over the female has led us to a continuous state of war, famine, poverty, a depleted Earth, a damaged ozone, the potential to blow up our planet a dozen times over. The list of sick situations is frightening.

The feminine energy must be brought to balance the untempered masculine. As woman rises from her oppressed condition, so man must fall from his unrealistic and destructive heights of power and control to meet the feminine half-way. Together, male and female, must produce a new way of being and give birth to a just and peaceful world.

The journey is long and painful, but we are responsible for making it. Together, men and women can do it. God—Mother and Father—is with us. The child is ours.

THE CHILD

Luke told this story and put it in his gospel. There's a priest called Zechariah. All the days of his life, he had been serving Yahweh. But he was depressed because he didn't have a child, and for a Jewish couple not to have children was really the pits. Poor old Zechariah, he'd been doing everything right, you see, but no babies. And so, one of these days when he is feeling particularly low, there in the sacristy, dutifully washing the chalices and fixing the candles, suddenly an angel appears to Zechariah. An angel by the name of Gabriel. Well, Zechariah drops the chalice, and his jaw hangs open, because he had never seen an angel before.

And the angel said, "Don't be afraid. I have some great news for you, great news. You're going to have a baby!" Well, the priest has a real problem, because he *knows* that's absurd. After all, he's been trying for years. But how do you communicate with an angel on the subject of the menopause? Zechariah's wife, Elizabeth, you see, she's a hundred! There's no way Elizabeth could have a child. So faithful old Zechariah is trying to say to the angel:

"Excuse me, Gabriel. I don't know what you do up there in Heaven, or wherever you've come from, but down here, you see, women go through these stages, and there's the menopause and my wife is..." Well, he's not getting through, right? Gabriel stands there saying,

"Come on, come on! Will you or will you not believe me!" But Zechariah, no he can't buy it!

In the end, Gabriel gets really angry and says: "You will be struck dumb until you see the Kingdom break through!" With which, off she goes, leaving Zechariah bewildered and dumb.

In the same chapter of Luke's gospel, there's a little lady, sitting in the kitchen doing her knitting, minding her own business, bothering nobody. And suddenly Gabriel appears to her and says, "Hail Mary!" And Mary drops her knitting because she hasn't seen an angel in a long time, and she's in a bit of a shock. "Don't be frightened, Mary. Don't be frightened. I have some terrific news for you. How about a new birth? How about a baby?"

Well, Mary is frozen at that point. She says, "Oh, my God! A baby!" And she has a similar problem to Zechariah. How do you communicate with an angel, a vision, about sexual intercourse? Because, you see, she hasn't been with a man, and, as we all well know, unless you've been with a man, you can't have a baby. So Mary tries to explain to the angel. "Well...look Gabriel, thanks very much and all that, but it's just not possible because the circumstances and the situation is..."

Gabriel is standing next to Mary, getting a little frustrated. "Come on now, for God's sake! Will you or won't you say Yes?" And then a naughty gleam comes in Mary's eyes, and she says to herself,

"Why not? *Why not?* Oooh!" I think that for Mary, it suddenly became a marvelous possibility. I don't think she quietly whispered, 'Oh yes, angel,

be it done to me according to thy word.' Be *real!*
She probably said, "Why *not?* Yes, I'll go for it!"
And away flits Gabriel...

Imagine what it must have been like that night
for Mary. She's there at home, making omelettes or
whatever. Joseph, is coming for dinner, and Mary is
waiting for him. Joseph is a carpenter, so he's hot
and sweaty, and he's had a long day at the lumber
yard, so he's tired.

Enter Joseph. Mary says as brightly as she can,
"Hello, Joe. Would you like a cup of coffee?
Emmm...a drop of Scotch? Two shots of Scotch?"
Pause.
"Uh, Joseph, I've something to tell you."
"Alright, what's that, love?"
"Um, Joseph, I'm pregnant!"
"What?" Splutters Joseph, "You're *pregnant!*"
"Y-yeah. I'm having a baby."

Can you imagine what Joseph is going through?
Well, he's furious! And Mary says, "N-no, just sit
down Joseph. Listen to me! This is what happened...
I was sitting in the kitchen doing my knitting,
minding my own business, when an angel appeared
and..."
"Oh yeah?" Joseph looks at her as though she's
gone nuts. "Woman! That's it. I quit. I'm finished
with you!"

Off he goes, stomp-stomp-stomp back to his
mother, he leaves her. He's furious. And in the
Gospel of Matthew, the first chapter, Joseph goes to

bed in his mother's house, and he falls asleep. An angel appears (you do believe in angels, don't you?) And begins with the same words: "Do not be afraid. You must go back to the woman. You must believe what the woman says, for she has within her a new possibility, the New Life. Do not be afraid."

The great thing about Joseph is not, as they say, that he was celibate, nor that he was supportive, but that he was humble enough and honest enough to return to Mary and say, "I will walk with you. I don't understand all of this, I don't know what is happening, but I will walk with you. I will be your partner in the birthing of a new possibility. We will share everything." And that's what Joseph did. He went back to the woman to support her in her crazy, ridiculous birthing process.

The story moves on. In the gospel of Luke, there's a bunch of farmers and peasants in the fields, simple folk who never got a degree, never went to university. Probably high-school drop-outs. And there they were, taking care of their sheep and goats, when suddenly, in the heavens —not one this time, but a whole crowd of angels appeared with trumpets blaring. And they were singing: "Good news! We have good news for you!" And the shepherds say,

"Ooh! What's that?"

"There's a baby. There's a new thing coming into being. There's a new possibility!" And do you know? Those silly, simple shepherds said,

"Really? Where is it? Show us. Where is it?" They didn't ask anything else, they simply wanted to know which way to go. And Gabriel said,

"Do you see that big star shining over there? Follow it!" And those shepherds, those simple people, they took some of their sheep, but not all, and they set out on their journey, following the new star that arose in the East.

Later on, in the gospel of Luke, there is a man walking by the lake. He sees the men and women in their boats, and they have all their nets tangled up, they're having a terrible time sorting through all the knots and tears. And the man comes and says to them, "Let go and follow me!" First they had to get untangled. But do you know? They let go of the nets, of all that bound them and tied them down, and they stood up and they followed him. I guess it was like flying out of the jar.

And some folks are doing it today.

But, probably, they are not normal.

MORE READING

I am well aware that this little book, which is based on talks I have given at various places over the past three or four years, can only touch on some of the issues involved in reaching the point of flying out of the jar. If you are a reader, you may find the following booklist helpful, as I have.

Adam, Eve and the Serpent
Elaine Pagels   Random House   1989

The Chalice and the Blade *Our History, Our Future*
Riane Eisler   Harper San Francisco   1988

The Crone *Women of Age, Wisdom & Power*
Barbara Walker   Harper San Francisco   1988

Exploring the Feminine Face of God
B. M. Meehan   Sheed & Ward   1991

The Goddess Within
A Guide to Eternal Myths that Shape Women's Lives
Woolger   Fawcett Columbine   1989

The Gospel According to Mary
Miriam T. Winter   Crossroads   1993

The Great Cosmic Mother
Sjoo & Mor   Harper San Francisco   1987

I Hear A Seed Growing *God of the Forest, God of the Streets*
Edwina Gateley   Source Books   1990

Illuminations of Hildegaard of Bingen
Matthew Fox, Ed.   Bear & Co.   1985

In Memory of Her
A Feminist Reconstruction of Christian Origins
E. S. Fiorenza   Crossroads   1984

Julian of Norwich: Showings
Cooledge   Paulist Press   1988

A Land Flowing with Milk & Honey
Perspectives on Feminist Theology
Moltmann–Wendell   Crossroads   1988

Meditations with Hildegaard of Bingen
Gabriel Unlein   Bear & Co.   1983

Meditations with Julian of Norwich
Brendan Doyle   Bear & Co.   1983

Meditations with Mechtild of Magdeburg
Sue Woodruff   Bear & Co.   1982

Meditations with Meister Eckhart
Matthew Fox   Bear & Co.   1983

Original Blessing *A Primer in Creation Spirituality*
Matthew Fox   Bear & Co.   1990

Psalms of A Laywoman
Edwina Gateley   Source Books   1988

Revelations of Divine Love of Julian of Norwich
James Walsh, Ed.   Anthony Clarke   1978

The Serpent and the Goddess
Mary Condren   Harper Collins   1989

Sexism and God–talk *Towards a Feminist Theology*
Rosemary Radford Ruether   Beacon Press   1983

Song of the Bird
Anthony De Mello   Doubleday   1984

When God was a Woman
Merlin Stone   Harcourt   1978

Wisdom's Feast
Cady, Ronan, Tanssig   Harper Collins   1989

Woman Wisdom
Miriam T. Winter   Crossroads   1991

Woman Witness
Miriam T. Winter   Crossroads   1992

Women Who Run With Wolves
C. Pinkola Estes   Ballantine   1992

EDWINA GATELEY

Born in Lancaster, England, Edwina has a teaching credential and a Masters Degree in Theological Studies. In the 1960s she worked in Uganda where she established a school for girls which became one of the most successful in the region. She went on to found the Volunteer Missionary Movement to prepare lay missionaries for work in the developing world. The VMM now has communities in Britain, Ireland, and the USA, and has sent over 1000 people to Africa, Papua New Guinea and South America.

In 1981 Edwina spent nine months of prayer and solitude in a hermitage in Illinois. This led her to the streets of Chicago, where for a year she walked with the homeless, the dispossessed, and women in prostitution. By 1984, she was able to found Genesis House, Chicago where women who are victims of prostitution and other abuse are welcomed and can feel safe, and where they can grow in self-respect and dignity. A second house for long–term care opened in Chicago in 1995.

Edwina's work has gained her recognition from many places: Catholic Woman of 1979 in England and Wales; The Spirit of St. Francis Award; The U.S. Catholic Mission Award; The Pope John XXIII Award, and so on. She is currently engaged in writing, advocating for women in prostitution, and conducting workshops, conferences and retreats in Britain, the U.S. and several other countries. Her publications include: *Psalms of A Laywoman* 1981, *I Hear A Seed Growing* 1990, a children's book: *God Goes on Vacation* 1995, and *There Was No Path, So I Trod One*, 1996. All are available from religious bookshops or from Source Books.

For information about speaking engagements, please write to

Maureen Donnelly
248 Carroll Ave. S.E.
Grand Rapids MI 49506